Mitchel

WILLIAM ZINSSER

Foreword by Albert Murray

 PAUL DRY BOOKS

Philadelphia   2000

Mitchell &Ruff

An American Profile in Jazz

First Paul Dry Books Edition, 2000

Paul Dry Books, Inc.
Philadelphia, Pennsylvania
www.pauldrybooks.com

Text type: Galliard
Display type: Isbell Family/Adobe Garamond
Composed by Duke & Company
Designed by Adrianne Onderdonk Dudden

1 3 5 7 9 10 8 6 4 2
Printed in the United States of America

Library of Congress Cataloging-in-Publication Data
Zinsser, William Knowlton.
    Mitchell & Ruff : an American profile in jazz / William Zinsser ; foreword by
Albert Murray.—1st Paul Dry Books ed.
        p. cm.
    Originally published: Willie and Dwike. New York : Harper & Row, 1984.
    ISBN 0-9664913-4-3 (pbk. : alk. paper)
    1. Mitchell, Dwike. 2. Ruff, Willie. 3. Jazz musicians—United States—Biography.
I. Title: Mitchell and Ruff. II. Title.
ML395 .Z56 2000
781.65'092'2—dc21   00-064665

CD available at www.willieruff.com

Contents

Foreword . . . *by Albert Murray*

To my delight, this book is remarkably free of social science findings and studies and speculations about race relations. Its fundamental concern is with the development of an American esthetic sensibility. The author, William Zinsser, wants to find out how that sensibility was formed, and that leads him to approach Dwike Mitchell and Willie Ruff as artists. He isn't thrown off by issues of politics and justice and injustice. What he's after is how an American personality develops. There's something about these two musicians that attracted him to them. He wants to know: Where did they come from and how did they get to be where they were when I encountered them? What enables them to play music that I admire so much?

John A. Kouwenhoven, in his book *Made In America,* talks about what's particularly American about American culture. He suggests that it's a mixture of learned traditions imported by emigrants from Europe with native or frontier forms, which together create the vernacular. That combination in turn gets refined, beyond folk, beyond pop, into the most comprehensive forms of fine art. You can find the 12-bar blues stanza of a Mississippi delta guitarist, for example, elaborated into an American sonata form known as the jazz instrumental in Duke Ellington's "Harlem Air Shaft." The process has nothing to do with social status. It's a matter of how artists develop a growing mastery of their medium.

In *Mitchell & Ruff*, Zinsser never loses sight of that process. He focuses on why Dwike Mitchell plays the piano as he does, and why Willie Ruff plays the bass and the French horn as he does. He discovers that their music is a fusion of what was imported to this country and what evolved here. Everything he learns about the life of the two musicians reaffirms that dynamic. Mitchell realizes as a young man that the piano is his destiny. The more he learns about it, the more he wants to learn about it. He wants to know what a piano is, and what has been done with it, and therefore what *he* can do with it—what he can say with the piano about his experience. He can say more if he knows what other people have done with piano keys, so there's everything possible to be learned. His whole life becomes a search for what will make him a better artist. The same is true of Willie Ruff. He goes wherever he needs to go to learn what he wants to know next: to Yale to study with Paul Hindemith, to Africa to study the drum language of the Pygmies, to St. Mark's church in Venice to listen for "a distant sound."

Zinsser stays focused on that double search. He goes down to Florida and Alabama, where Mitchell and Ruff grew up—which is a long way from his own hometown of New York. But he doesn't confuse what he finds with exotica. He never forgets that he's dealing with American character and how it gets shaped into art. Being a down-home boy myself, from Alabama, I feel a connection between Mitchell and Ruff's early years and my own early years as I describe them in my novel *Train Whistle Guitar*. The novel is about a little boy growing up on the outskirts of Mobile, listening to the guitar players and juke-joint piano players and becoming a serious schoolboy. I was that schoolboy, developing literary and intellectual interests at an early age and going on to win scholarships, right through college. Mitchell and Ruff did it in a different way. I did it through literature and they did it through music, but they achieved the same level of sophistication in their chosen métier. Their way was more improvisational—their first conservatory was an air force base in Ohio—but for all three of us it was the same picaresque fairy tale.

The similarity really hit me when Dwike Mitchell talks about how he was made to play the piano in the Baptist church when he was a small boy in Florida and how the minister would preach about how everyone would be damned and go to Hell. What he says is very close to what I say about Sunday mornings in *Train Whistle Guitar:* "The sermons used to be so full not only of ugly prophecies and warnings but also outright threats of divine vengeance on hypocrites that when people all around you began stomping and clapping and shouting you couldn't tell whether they were doing so because they were being visited by the Holy Ghost or because being grown folks and therefore accountable for their trespasses they were even more terrified of the dreadful wrath of God than you were (whose sins after all were still being charged against your parents)."

The point is that I feel a close personal identification with Zinsser's portrayal of Mitchell and Ruff, not just because I'm from the South, but because his book is an excellent natural history of the development of our sensibility as indigenous American artists. The book has nothing to do with race relations as such. Zinsser has an omni-American sensibility —it's neither white nor black. That sensibility is also at the heart of my work. I never think of myself as an "African-American." As Willie Ruff says to the old monsignor in St. Mark's church, it's a word I don't use.

Mitchell & Ruff is the literary equivalent of a jazz piece. It's composed, it has themes, and it develops those themes. Zinsser's prose tries to get as close as possible to the rhythms these two men use in their music. To me the *ur*-father of jazz in prose is Ernest Hemingway. Hemingway swings; his prose is as precise as it is lyrical. What he did is exactly what Count Basie thought you should do when you're playing music: Don't use frills or curlicues; get a good solid rhythm; make it swing. That's what Zinsser does. He tells his story with a directness and a simplicity that add up to the kind of elegance that the higher physicists admire.

Zinsser sees Mitchell and Ruff just about as I would see them. That impressed me, because he's a Yankee, working in a context he's not as intimate with as I am. Ordinarily when people enter an unfamiliar situation there are two common reactions. One is insecurity, which results in xenophobia: fear, or hostility, or condescension. The other is to see the situation as exotic, or weird, or dangerous, and to find it fascinating—as all those people did who used to go slumming in Harlem. But here's a man who identifies with Mitchell and Ruff because their story is universal, and he's sensitive to the local conventions that an outsider needs to penetrate in order to tell that story. He doesn't allow anything to get in the way of the relationship—the kinship—of these two men from the South.

So what you've got in *Mitchell & Ruff* is not only a profile of two people but, in effect, a profile of three people: Dwike Mitchell and Willie Ruff and William Zinsser. I'm completely comfortable with Zinsser's take on the down-home neighborhoods he visited. He never got deflected from what he wrote this book to find out: how these two men forged their American identity as artists. It pleases me that he chose to move into this context and that he wrote about it so well.

1 ... Shanghai

Jazz came to China for the first time on the afternoon of June 2, 1981, when the American bassist and French-horn player Willie Ruff introduced himself and his partner, the pianist Dwike Mitchell, to several hundred students and professors who were crowded into a large room at the Shanghai Conservatory of Music. The students and the professors were all expectant, without knowing quite what to expect. They only knew that they were about to hear the first American jazz concert ever presented to the Chinese. Probably they were not surprised to find that the two musicians were black, though black Americans are a rarity in the People's Republic. What they undoubtedly didn't expect was that Ruff would talk to them in Chinese, and when he began they murmured with delight.

Ruff is a lithe, dapper man in his early fifties who takes visible pleasure in sharing his enthusiasms, and it was obvious that there was no place he would rather have been than in China's oldest conservatory, bringing the music of his people to still another country deprived of that commodity. In 1959 he and Mitchell—who have played together as the Mitchell-Ruff Duo for almost thirty years—introduced jazz to the

Soviet Union, and for that occasion Ruff taught himself Russian, his seventh language. In 1979 he hit on the idea of making a similar trip to China, and he began taking intensive courses in Chinese at Yale, where he is a professor of music. By the winter of 1981 he felt that he was fluent enough in Mandarin to make the trip.

Now Ruff stood at the front of the room surveying the Chinese faces. He looked somewhat like an Oriental sage himself—or at least like the traditional carving of one; he is the color of old ivory, with a bald head and the beginnings of a Mandarin beard. He was holding several sheets of paper on which he had written, in Chinese characters, what he wanted to tell his listeners about the origins of jazz.

"In the last three hundred and fifty years," he began, "black people in America have created a music that is a rich contribution to Western culture. Of course three hundred and fifty years, compared to the long and distinguished history of Chinese music, seems like only a moment. But please remember that the music of American black people is an amalgam whose roots are deep in African history and also that it has taken many characteristics from the music of Europe."

Ruff has an amiable voice, and as he declaimed the first sentences, relishing the swoops and cadences of his latest adopted language, he had already established contact with the men and women in the room. They were attentive but relaxed —not an audience straining to decipher a foreigner's accent.

"In Africa the drum is the most important musical instrument," Ruff went on. "But to me the intriguing thing is that the people also use their drums to talk. Please imagine that the drum method of speech is so exquisite that Africans can, without recourse to words, recite proverbs, record history and send long messages. The drum is to West African society what the book is to literate society."

I wondered what the audience would make of that. Not only was China the oldest of literate societies; we were in the one Asian city that was encrusted with Western thought as transmitted in books, in journals and in musical notation—a city whose symphony orchestra, when it was founded in 1922, consisted entirely of Europeans. Even the architecture of Shanghai was a patchwork of Western shapes—a residue of the days when the city had a huge foreign population and was divided into districts that were controlled by different European countries. At the conservatory we were in the former French concession, and its main building was in a red brick French provincial style, with a sloping red tile roof and a porte cochere. Another French-style building housed the conservatory's library of 100,000 books about music—definitely not the oral tradition. Newer buildings served as classrooms and practice rooms, and the music that eddied out of their windows was the dreary fare of Western academic rigor: vocal scales endlessly rising, piano arpeggios repeated until they were mastered, chamber groups starting and stopping and starting again. We could have been in Vienna of the nineties or Paris of the twenties. In any case, we were a long way from Africa. And we were farther still from music created spontaneously.

"In the seventeenth century," Ruff continued, "when West Africans were captured and brought to America as slaves, they brought their drums with them. But the slave owners were afraid of the drum because it was so potent; it could be used to incite the slaves to revolt. So they outlawed the drum. This very shrewd law had a tremendous effect on the development of black people's music. Our ancestors had to develop a variety of drum substitutes. One of them, for example, was tap dancing—I'm sure you've all heard of that. Now I'd like to show you a drum substitute that you probably don't know about, one that uses the hands and the body to make rhythm. It's called hambone."

There was no translating "hambone" into Mandarin—the odd word hung in the air. But Ruff quickly had an intricate rhythm going, slapping himself with the palms of his hands and smacking his open mouth to create a series of resonating pops. Applause greeted this proof that the body could be its own drum.

"By the time jazz started to develop," Ruff went on, "all African instruments in America had disappeared. So jazz borrowed the instruments of Western music, like the ones we're playing here today." He went over to his own instrument, the bass, and showed how he used it as a percussion instrument by picking the strings with his fingers instead of playing them with a bow. "Only this morning," he said, "I gave a lesson to your distinguished professor of bass, and he is already *very good.*"

Moving from rhythm to terrain that was more familiar

to his listeners, he pointed out that jazz took its structural elements from European harmony. "Mr. Mitchell will now give you an example of the music that American slaves found in the Christian churches—Protestant hymns that had been brought from Europe. Slaves were encouraged to embrace Christianity and to use its music. Please listen."

Mitchell played an old Protestant hymn. "The slaves adopted these harmonies and transformed them into their own very emotional spirituals," Ruff said. "Mr. Mitchell and I will sing you a famous Negro spiritual from the days of slavery. It's called 'My Lord, What a Morning.'" With Mitchell playing a joyful accompaniment, the two men sang five or six choruses of the lovely old song, Mitchell carrying the melody in his deep voice, Ruff taking the higher second part. The moment, musically beautiful, had an edge of faraway sadness. I couldn't help thinking of another alien culture onto which the Protestant hymns of Europe had once been strenuously grafted. It was just beyond the conservatory gates.

"Mr. Mitchell will now show you how the piano can be used as a substitute for the instruments of the orchestra," Ruff said. "Please notice that he uses his left hand to play the bass and also to make his rhythm section. Later he will use his right hand to play the main melody and to fill in the harmony. This style is called ragtime." Mitchell struck up a jaunty rag. The students perked up at the playful pattern of the notes. Ruff looked out at his class and beamed. The teacher in him was beginning to slip away; the musician in him was tugging at his sleeve and telling him to start the concert.

. . .

I have known Willie Ruff and Dwike Mitchell since 1973, when I became master of Branford College at Yale. Ruff also lived in the college, as a resident fellow. He had recently persuaded Yale to hold a convocation at which forty of America's greatest black musicians were honored and were named Duke Ellington Fellows. They included Ellington himself, Dizzy Gillespie, Odetta, Charlie Mingus, Benny Carter, Slam Stewart, Bessie Jones, William Warfield, Marian Anderson, Roland Hayes, Paul Robeson, Honi Coles—in short, the pantheon of black composers, instrumentalists, arrangers, singers and dancers.

Ruff's idea had two components. One was that Yale should recognize "the conservatory without walls," as he calls the informal system whereby black musicians hand their heritage down. The other was that the Ellington Fellows would come to New Haven periodically to play for Yale students and for the pupils of the city's predominantly black public schools. Over the subsequent years Ruff shepherded these giants through our lives. First they would give a concert for New Haven schoolchildren in a Yale auditorium; then Ruff would trot them into his own classes and out to various city schools. The musicians, far from wilting, blossomed. Their life work had been almost obliterated by three social forces that coincided in the 1960s: the rise of rock, the death of nightclubs because of television, and the exclusion of black performers from network TV. Now they were old and the hour was late. Facing a generation that didn't even know they existed, they summoned ancient reserves of energy and skill.

While Ruff's stars came and went, the same person was always at the piano—a large black man with a shy smile, who never said anything and didn't have to. His piano said it all. However disparate the visiting musicians might be, he was sensitive to their tradition. Dwike Mitchell was the best jazz pianist I had heard in all my years of listening to pianists I admired—players like Cy Walter, Bill Evans, Oscar Peterson, George Shearing, and Ellis Larkins—and trying to find their sophisticated chords on my own piano. Mitchell's harmonies were elegant and stunning, his technique was awesome, his taste impeccable. I became a Mitchell addict. Whenever he came up from New York to play with Ruff in a concert or a class I was there, sitting where I could watch his big and miraculous hands.

But what gave me my affection for Mitchell and Ruff was that they seemed to be under some moral persuasion to pass their experience along. I wanted to know who had stamped this idea on them. What teachers had crossed their own lives when they were growing up in small Southern towns?

They met in 1947 when they were servicemen at Lockbourne Air Force Base, outside Columbus, Ohio. Mitchell, then seventeen and a pianist in the unit band, needed an accompanist, and he gave the newly arrived Ruff, a sixteen-year-old French-horn player, a crash course in playing the bass. Thus the Mitchell-Ruff Duo was unofficially born.

When they were discharged they followed separate paths and lost contact. Mitchell went to the Philadelphia Musical Academy. Ruff went to the Yale School of Music, where he studied with Paul Hindemith. Venturing out with his master's degree in 1954, he was told that no American symphony orchestra would hire a black musician, and he accepted an offer to join the Tel Aviv Symphony as first French horn. Shortly before he was to leave he happened to turn his television set on to *The Ed Sullivan Show.* Lionel Hampton's band was playing, and as the camera panned over to the piano Ruff saw a familiar figure at the keyboard. Mitchell, it turned out, had been Hampton's pianist for the past two years. Ruff telephoned him backstage at the CBS studio; Mitchell hinted at imminent vacancies in the brass section. A few days later Israel lost—and Hampton got—a superb French horn.

The Mitchell-Ruff Duo—"the oldest continuous group in jazz without personnel changes," Ruff says—was officially formed in 1955 when the two men left Hampton and struck out on their own. They were booked regularly by the major nightclubs as the second act with the great bands of the day: Louis Armstrong, Duke Ellington, Dizzy Gillespie, Miles Davis. "They were our mentors," Ruff recalls. "They'd play a set and then we'd play a set and they'd hang around and tell us what we could be doing better. We learned everything from those men. Count Basie's band raised us. In 1956 they were the hottest band in the country—they were the most expensive band and we were the cheapest—and we sold out Birdland every night. One evening Miles Davis brought Billie

Holiday in to hear us and we just about fell through the floor. We were just kids."

Meanwhile they caught the attention of another group of patrons—one at the opposite end of music's social scale. It was a group of older women in New York who had formed an organization called Young Audiences to introduce elementary school and high school students to chamber music. For their teachers the women chose young professionals who could communicate with words as well as with music, and Mitchell and Ruff were the first people they selected to teach jazz. "It was done," Ruff recalls, "under the supervision of the founders—Mrs. Lionello Perera, a great patron of music, and Mrs. Edgar Leventritt, who started the Leventritt Competition—and Nina Collier and several other ladies who sat on the board. They taught us definite techniques, such as how to catch the attention of children, and they also gave us lessons in grooming and enunciation and conduct. They were very stern and really quite unpleasant, but instructive. Everything they told us turned out to be true."

Armed with these graces, Mitchell and Ruff hit the road for Young Audiences, often giving seven or eight performances a day, going from school to school, first in New York and later in Boston, Baltimore and San Francisco. They also did a tour of Indian schools in New Mexico. The Duo alternated these forays with its stands in Manhattan clubs. Then, in 1959, it made its famous trip to Russia. Ruff arranged the trip himself with Soviet officials after the State Department, which had been trying for two years to get Louis Armstrong into the Soviet Union, declined to help. In Russia the two Americans—playing and teaching for five weeks at conservatories in Leningrad, Moscow, Kiev, Yalta, Sochi and Riga—found a thirst for jazz that surprised even them. When they left Moscow, nine hundred people turned up at the train station to see them off and throw flowers into their compartment. Mitchell, in turn, still remembers being moved by many Russian songs that resembled spirituals he had heard in the black churches of his boyhood. Whether a scholar could find any such link doesn't matter to him; in music he operates on an emotional level that has no need for evidence. "I felt a mysterious bond between their people and my people," he says. "I think I connected with their suffering."

Not long after that, the house of jazz began to crumble. Television was the new medium and rock the new musical message. "Nightclubs started closing in the very early sixties," Ruff recalls. "The number of jazz performers who quit, died or just disappeared was astounding. Many of them moved to Europe. Three of the greatest rhythm players—Oscar Pettiford, Bud Powell and Kenny Clarke—were living in Paris and playing for peanuts because they couldn't find any work in the United States. How devastating it was for us to play in Europe and see so many of these great men so reduced!" Mitchell and Ruff survived because of their teaching bent. They had caught the attention of two venerable booking agencies, Pryor-Menz and Alkahest, that wanted a young act to give jazz concerts for college audiences and also explain the music. Thereby they found the format—sixty or seventy concerts a year, mainly at colleges—that has been their main source of income to this day.

A new tool came their way in 1967 when CBS Television sent them to Brazil to make a one-hour film tracing the African roots of Brazilian music. Ruff saw the value of film as a teaching device and went back to college to study film. Since then he has visited Bali, Senegal and the Pygmies of the Central African Republic to make films about the drum music and drum language of those societies. He always came back to Yale elated by new rhythmical affinities that he had found among diverse cultures and among seemingly unrelated forms of life. His seminars on rhythm began to make startling connections as he brought Yale professors into them from such disciplines as neurology, geology, limnology, art, English, astronomy, physiology and physics. The professors became almost as excited as Ruff.

Maybe I should have guessed that Ruff would want to introduce jazz to China. But his projects always took me by surprise because they reflected still another interest I hadn't known about. He is a man on the move, a listener and a learner, a hustler and a charmer, making his own luck. Mitchell, by contrast, seemed during those years at Yale to be withdrawn and laconic. But when I moved back to New York in 1979 I asked if he would take me on as a piano student, and he turned out to be a man of warmth and humor. Still, he is glad to leave life's arrangements to someone who enjoys making them. He stays in his New York apartment, practicing from morning to night, until Ruff calls and tells him where they are going next. As he has discovered, it could be Senegal or Shanghai.

"If it sounds right to me," he says, "I just tell him, 'O.K., Ruff, let's go.'"

. . .

We flew to Shanghai on a Chinese 747—Ruff walked up and down the aisles trying out his Chinese on the passengers—and the next day we called on Professor Tan Shu-chen, deputy director of the Shanghai Conservatory of Music, who was, so far, our only contact. Originally, Ruff had sought the sponsorship of the Center for United States–China Arts Exchange, the group that was sending American musicians to China, but his letter got no answer. Ruff felt that no matter how many great American artists went to China—Isaac Stern, the Boston Symphony Orchestra, Roberta Peters—the music that they played and sang would be European music. The indigenous music of America was jazz, and the Chinese had never heard it in a live performance. (When Ruff asked a Chinese man on the plane whether his people were familiar with jazz, he said, "Oh, yes, we know Stephen Foster very well.") Lacking official support, Ruff decided to go anyway. He booked himself and Mitchell on a two-week tour to Shanghai and Peking, the two cities that had major conservatories, and then went looking for money. He got a grant from Coca-Cola that would cover their expenses and the costs of filming their visit.

To have Professor Tan as our host was all that we could

have asked. He had come to New York the previous winter in connection with the Academy Award–winning film *From Mao to Mozart—Isaac Stern in China,* in which he describes his imprisonment during China's Cultural Revolution. Ruff invited him to visit the Yale School of Music, in the long-range hope of fostering some kind of collaboration that would help both institutions—an exchange of students or teachers or manuscripts between Yale and the Shanghai Conservatory. While Professor Tan was at Yale he attended a class in which Ruff and Mitchell were playing, and he invited them, in turn, to visit his conservatory. That was all that a born improviser needed to hear. Now we were at the conservatory, and Professor Tan was showing us around. He had arranged the jazz concert for the next afternoon.

The Shanghai Conservatory of Music, which was founded in 1927 and which prides itself on being part of the cultural conscience of China, has 650 students—the youngest are eight years old—and 300 teachers. Most of the students live on the campus. Quite a few are from Shanghai, but a large number are recruited from all over China by faculty members, who hold regional auditions.

The conservatory has five departments of instruction—piano; voice; strings and winds; composing and conducting; and traditional Chinese instruments—and two of musicology. One of these is a musical research institute. The other, devoted to Chinese traditional and folk music, was recently formed to broaden the conservatory's involvement with the heritage of its own country. But the tilt is definitely Westward. Most of the conservatory's original teachers were Europeans, and many of its graduates have lived in the West and won recognition there. The curriculum, from what I could hear of it, was rooted in Europe: Bach, Scarlatti, Mozart, Beethoven, Brahms, Schubert, Chopin, Verdi. The biggest class that we saw consisted of a forty-piece student orchestra, led by a student conductor, playing Dvořák's Cello Concerto.

Professor Tan was a product of this tradition—and was one of its first casualties when the Cultural Revolution struck. He was born in 1907, and as a boy he studied violin privately with Dutch and Italian teachers who were living in China. When he joined the Shanghai Municipal Orchestra, in 1927, he was its first Chinese member. He recalls the conductor, an Italian named Mario Paci, as a man of such fierce temper that he constantly broke his baton. Thus he learned at an early age that one of the liveliest currents running through Western music is high emotion among its practitioners.

In 1929 Professor Tan turned to teaching—at one point he was teaching violin at six different colleges in Shanghai—and he rejoined the symphony in 1937. By that time it had four Chinese members; obviously Shanghai was still a creature of the West, its white population continuing to dream of a world that would never change. Pearl Harbor put an end to that reverie. During World War II the Japanese occupied Shanghai, foreigners were interned in concentration camps, and the colonizing grip of the West was finally pried loose.

It was no time or place for a musician to earn a living—"one month's salary would buy one shoe," Professor Tan recalled—and, seeking a more practical trade, he went to architecture school and earned his degree. He returned to music after the war, however, joining the Shanghai Conservatory in 1947 and becoming its deputy director in 1949, when the Communists came to power. The school thereupon began its biggest era of growth. The student body expanded and European music regained its hold. But the older students were also required to go away and work for three months every year on farms and in factories.

"The peasants and workers disliked Western music because it belonged to the rich people," Professor Tan told me. "And our students couldn't practice much because they met so much criticism. Here at the conservatory we never knew where we stood. Periods of criticism would alternate with periods of relaxation. It was an uneasy time. In fact, just before the Cultural Revolution I was thinking of retiring from teaching. I had a sense of a coming storm. We are like animals—we can feel that."

The storm broke on June 5, 1966. The first winds of the Cultural Revolution hit the conservatory from within. "On the first day, posters were put up and meetings were held denouncing the director, Professor Ho Lu-ting," Professor Tan said. "The next day the attack was aimed at me. I was accused of poisoning the minds of the students. My crime was that I was teaching Mozart. I happen to be a blind admirer of European and American people and music and culture, so everything I had been teaching was poison. Bach and Beethoven were poison. And Brahms. And Paganini.

"At first it was only posters and meetings. Then the conservatory was closed and much of our music was destroyed. We were beaten every day by students and by young people who came in from outside. Boys of ten or eleven would throw stones at us. They really believed we were bad people—especially any professor who was over forty. The older you were, the worse you were. For a year, more than a hundred of us older teachers were beaten and forced to spend every day shut up together in a closed shed. Then there was a year when we had to do hard labor. Ten professors died from the strain; one of them had a heart attack when a young guard made him run after him for a mile. He just dropped dead at the end.

"Then came the solitary confinement. Our director was kept in prison, in chains, for five years. I was put in the worst room they could find here—a very small room in the basement, hardly any bigger than my bed. It had no light and no windows, and it was smelly because it was next to a septic tank, and there was nothing to do to pass the time. I was kept there for fourteen months."

In 1971 Professor Tan was allowed to go home to live with his family, pending the verdict on his "crimes," but he still had to do physical labor at the conservatory during the day. Finally, in 1976, the Gang of Four was overthrown, the professors were declared innocent, and the conservatory reopened. Professor Tan told me that among the students he readmitted were many who had beaten and tormented him. I said that I could hardly imagine such forbearance. "I didn't think about that," he said. "The past is the past."

Professor Tan is a small, gentle man with white hair and a modest manner. He dresses in the informal work clothes that everybody wears in Shanghai; nobody would take him for one of the city's cultural eminences. He moves somewhat slowly and has fairly strong glasses—marks, perhaps, of his long captivity. "The students have made astonishing progress since 1976," he told me, "because now they can play whole-heartedly. I love being able to teach the violin again. It's such an enjoyment to hear people who are truly talented. Yesterday a girl played the 'Scottish Fantasy' of Max Bruch, and although I was supposed to be teaching her I only sat and listened and never said a word. It was just right."

He was equally pleased by the thought of bringing jazz to his students. "I've never seen any jazz musicians in China," he said. "Nobody here knows anything about jazz. When I heard Mr. Ruff and Mr. Mitchell play at Yale I realized that it was very important music. I wanted my teachers and my students to hear it. I wanted them to know what real American jazz is like."

. . .

When Mitchell finished his ragtime tune the audience clapped—apparently glad to hear some of the converging elements that Ruff had talked about earlier. "Now," Ruff said, "we're going to give you an example of blues." It was another word that didn't lend itself to Mandarin, and it sounded unusually strung out: *blooooze.* "One of the fundamental principles of jazz is form," Ruff continued, "and blues are a perfect illustration. Blues almost always have a twelve-bar form. This twelve-bar form never changes. It wouldn't change even if we stayed here and played it all night." He paused to let this sink in. "But you don't have to worry—we aren't going to play it that long." It was his first joke in Chinese, and it went over well. Mitchell then played an easygoing blues—a classic example of what came up the river from New Orleans, with a strong left hand ornamented by graceful runs in the right hand. Ruff joined in on his bass, and they played several twelve-bar choruses.

After that Ruff brought up the matter of improvisation, which he called "the lifeblood of jazz." He said that when he was young he worried because his people hadn't developed from their experience in America a written tradition of opera, like Chinese opera, that chronicled great or romantic events. "But later I stopped worrying because I saw that the master performers of our musical story—Louis Armstrong, Ella Fitzgerald and so many others—have enriched our culture with the beauty of what they created spontaneously. Now please listen one more time to the blues form, and count the measures along with me." He wanted his listeners to count, he said, because the rules of jazz require the improviser, however wild his melodic journeys, to repeat the harmonic changes that went into the first statement of the theme. "After you count with me a few times through, Mr. Mitchell will begin one of his famous improvisations."

Mitchell played a simple blues theme, emphasizing the chord changes, and Ruff counted the twelve bars aloud in

English. Mitchell then restated the theme, embroidering it slightly, and this time Ruff counted in Chinese: *"Yi, er, san, si, wu, liu, qi, ba . . ."* This so delighted the students that they forgot to join him. "I can't hear you," Ruff said, teacher fashion, but they kept quiet and enjoyed his climb up the numerical ladder. Mitchell then embarked on a series of improvisations, some constructed of Tatum-like runs, some built on strong chord progressions (he can move immense chord clusters up and down the keyboard). Next, Ruff took a chorus on the bass; then they alternated their improvised flights, moving in twelve-bar segments to an ending that seemed as inevitable as if they had played it a hundred times before.

Changing the mood, Ruff announced that Mitchell would play a song called "Yesterday." Jerome Kern's plaintive melody is hardly the stuff of traditional jazz, nor was Mitchell's rendition of it—a treatment of classical intricacy, closer to Rachmaninoff (one of his heroes) than to any jazz pianist. The students applauded with fervor. Staying in a relatively classical vein, Ruff switched to the French horn and the two men played Billy Strayhorn's "Lush Life" in a mood which was slow and lyrical, almost like a German *lied,* and which perhaps surprised the students with its lack of an obvious rhythm.

The next number was one that I didn't recognize. It moved at a bright tempo and had several engaging themes that were brought back by the piano or the French horn— the usual jazzmen's game of statement and response. Twice, Mitchell briefly introduced a contrapuntal motif that was a deliberate imitation of Bach, and each time it drew a ripple of amusement from the professors and the students. It was the first time they had heard a kind of music that they knew from their own studies.

"That number," Ruff said, "is called 'Shanghai Blues.' We just made it up." The audience buzzed with amazement and pleasure.

I had been watching the professors and the students during the concert. Their faces had the look of people watching the slow approach of some great natural force—a tornado or a tidal wave. They had been listening to music that their experience had not prepared them to understand. Two black men were playing long stretches of music without resorting to any printed notes. Yet they obviously hadn't memorized what they were playing; their music took unexpected turns, seemingly at the whim of the musicians, straying all over the keyboard and all over the landscape of Western tonality. Nevertheless there was order. Themes that had been abandoned came back in different clothes. If the key changed, as it frequently did, the two men were always in the same key. Often there was a playfulness between the two instruments, and always there was rapport. But if the two players were exchanging any signals, the message was too quick for the untrained eye.

From the quality of the listeners' attention I could tell that the music was holding them in a strong grip. Their minds seemed to be fully engaged. Their bodies, however, were not. Only three pairs of feet in the whole room were tapping—

Mitchell's, Ruff's and mine. Perhaps this was a Chinese characteristic, this stillness of listening. But beyond that, the music wasn't easy. It never again approached the overt syncopation of the ragtime that Mitchell had played early in the program; that was where the essential gaiety of jazz had been most accessible. Nor did it have the flat-out gusto that an earlier generation of black musicians might have brought to China—the thumping rhythms and simpler harmonies of a James P. Johnson or a Fats Waller.

It wasn't that Mitchell and Ruff were playing jazz that was pedantic or sedate; on the contrary, I have seldom heard Mitchell play with more exuberant shifts of energy. But the music was full of subtleties—even a Westerner accustomed to jazz would have been charmed by its subtlety and wit. I had to remind myself that the Chinese had heard no Western music of any kind from 1966 to 1976. A twenty-one-year-old student in the audience would only have begun to listen to composers like Mozart and Brahms within the past five years. The jazz he was hearing now was not so different as to be a whole new branch of music. Mitchell was clearly grounded in Bach and Chopin; Ruff's French horn had echoes of all the classical works—Debussy's "Rêverie," Ravel's "Pavane"—in which that instrument has such uncanny power to move us.

After "Shanghai Blues" Ruff invoked the ancient device of teachers who know they have been presenting too much material too fast. He asked for questions. The serious faces relaxed.

"Where do people go to study jazz in America?" a student wanted to know. "What kind of courses do they take?"

Ruff explained that jazz courses, where they existed at all, would be part of a broad college curriculum that included, say, languages and history and physics. "But, really, jazz isn't learned in universities or conservatories," he said. "It's music that is passed on by older musicians to those of us who are younger."

It was not a helpful answer. What kind of subject doesn't have its own academy? A shyness settled over the room, though the students seemed full of curiosity. Professor Tan got up and stood next to Ruff. "I urge you to ask questions," he said. "I can assure you that jazz has many principles that apply to your studies here. In fact, I have many questions myself."

An old professor stood up. "When you created 'Shanghai Blues' just now," he said, "did you have a form for it, or a logical plan?"

"I just started tapping my foot," Ruff replied, tapping his foot to reconstruct the moment. "And then I started to play the first thought that came into my mind with the horn. And Mitchell heard it. And he answered. And after that we heard and answered, heard and answered, heard and answered."

"But how can you ever play it again?" the old professor said.

"We never can," Ruff replied.

"That is beyond our imagination," the professor said. "Our students here play a piece a hundred times, or two hun-

dred times, to get it exactly right. You play something once—
something very beautiful—and then you just throw it away."

Now the questions tumbled out. What was most on the
students' minds quickly became clear: it was the mystery of
improvisation. (The Chinese don't even have a word for improvisation of this kind; Ruff translated it as "something created during the process of delivery.") All the questions poked
at this central riddle—"Could a Chinese person improvise?"
and "Could two strangers improvise together?" and "How
can you compose at such speed?"—and it was at this point
that Ruff took one question and turned it into a moment
that stood us all on our ear.

Was it really possible, a student wanted to know, to improvise on any tune at all—even one that the musicians had
never heard before?

Ruff's reply was casual. "I would like to invite one of the
pianists here to play a short traditional Chinese melody that
I'm sure we would not know," he said, "and we will make a
new piece based on that."

The room erupted in oohs and cheers. I caught a look
on Mitchell's face that said, "This time you've gone too far."
The students began to call the name of the young man they
wanted to have play. When they found him in the crowd he
was so diffident that he got down on the floor to keep from
being dragged out. But his friends dragged him out anyway,
and, regaining his aplomb, he walked to the piano and sat
down with the formality of a concert artist. He was about
twenty-two. Mitchell stood at one side, looking grave.

The young man played his melody beautifully and with great feeling. It seemed to be his own composition, unknown to the other people. It began with four chords of distinctively Chinese structure, moved down the scale in a stately progression, paused, turned itself around with a transitional figure of lighter weight, and then started back up, never repeating itself and finally resolving the theme with a suspended chord that was satisfying because it was so unexpected. It was a perfect small piece, about fourteen bars long. The student walked back to his seat and Mitchell went back to the piano. The room got very quiet.

Mitchell's huge hands hovered briefly over the keys, and then the young man's melody came back to him. It was in the same key; it had the same chords, slightly embellished near the end, and, best of all, it had the same mood. Having stated the theme, Mitchell broadened it the second time, giving it a certain majesty, coloring the student's chords with dissonances that were entirely apt; he gave the "Chinese" chords a jazz texture but still preserved their mood. Then Ruff joined him on his bass, and they took the melody through a number of variations, Mitchell giving it a whole series of new lives but never losing its integrity. I listened to his feat with growing excitement. For me it was the climax of years of marveling at his ear and at his sensitivity to the material at hand. The students were equally elated and astonished. For them it was the ultimate proof—because it touched their own heritage—that for a jazz improviser no point of departure is alien.

After that a few more questions were asked, and Mitchell and Ruff concluded with a Gershwin medley from *Porgy and Bess* and a genial rendition of "My Old Flame." Professor Tan thanked the two men and formally ended the concert. Then he went over to Mitchell and took his hands in his own. "You are an artist," he said.

Later I told Mitchell that I thought Ruff had given him an unduly nervous moment when he invited one of the students to supply a melody.

"Well, naturally I was nervous," he said, "because I didn't have any idea what to expect. But, you know, that boy phrased his piece *perfectly*. The minute he started to play I got his emotions. I understood exactly what he was feeling, and the rest was easy. The notes and the chords just fell into place."

2 ... Dunedin

Dwike Mitchell was born on February 14, 1930, in the small town of Dunedin, Florida, and was named Ivory Mitchell, Jr. For a born piano player to inherit the name Ivory would seem to be a sign that he was favored by the gods. But the grown man, starting his professional life at the keyboard, rejected the gift. "There was Ivory Joe Hunter and all these other Ivorys who played the piano," Mitchell says. "I always wanted to be a pianist, but without any of those gimmicks —people saying, 'Oh, *Ivory,* you play the ivories!' I hated that. So I decided to change my name. I talked to my mother and she thought of this 'Dwike' and wrote me and told me to use it."

Ivory Mitchell, Sr., worked for the town of Dunedin when Ivory, Jr., was a baby, and it was the son's good fortune that the father's main job was driving the garbage truck. "They tell me I used to sit in my high chair," Mitchell recalls, "and just sing and make up songs and tap my fingers in rhythm on the tray, until finally my father said he thought I was interested in playing the piano. So he found one. He used to find all these things when he was driving the truck, and one day when I was about three he came across this old piano that somebody had thrown out. He brought it home and it was really fantastic. Every note played—there wasn't a broken key on it. And it had those clefs carved in the wood, with cloth behind them. It was too big to fit along one wall, so it stuck out partly across the door. My cousin next door had taken piano lessons, and she came over and played a tune that we called 'Coon Shine Baby.' In the North they call it something else. She taught me the tune and I learned it in five or ten minutes. And that was the beginning of my career playing the piano."

Mitchell went public with that career—not voluntarily—when he was five. His mother, Lilla, had a good classical voice, and she needed someone to accompany her solos during the Sunday morning service at the Shiloh Missionary Baptist Church, one of two churches that served Dunedin's tiny black community, the other being the African Methodist Episcopal Church. "She would pick out her songs on the piano for me," Mitchell says, "and I'd play them right away because I could hear them." There was only one problem in having a five-year-old accompanist at church: somebody had to pick him up and put him on the piano stool.

At home, however, Mitchell's mother treated him like any other boy starting on the piano—she made him do scales and exercises. "I wanted to play things I thought I heard in my head," he recalls, "and the things my mother taught me were just not the things I wanted to hear. So I rebelled against everything she wanted me to do and we had terrible fights." When Mitchell was eight, his parents were suddenly divorced and his mother left. But that didn't end his days as a church pianist. On the contrary, his elders were glad to have someone in their midst who could play anything he could hear, and they enlisted him to play for the junior choir and then for the entire Sunday morning service. Those Sundays were to stretch on for the rest of his boyhood. "I played in that church until I was seventeen," he says. "It seemed like an eternity."

The basic harmonies that accompanied church hymns soon struck Mitchell as too basic, and he began to add notes to the chords to make them more interesting. But he didn't reckon with Baptist ideas about chords that are more interesting. "We had this minister named W. A. Harrison," he says. "I never knew what the 'W' or the 'A' meant. He was very strict about the music, and you played everything *exactly*. Anything else that you might play had something to do with the Devil. If you ever threw an extra note into a chord— maybe something you'd heard on the radio that you felt good about—Reverend Harrison would give you the old eye.

"There was one Sunday I'll never forget. Church services were so long—oh, they were so long. We'd go to church at eleven and we didn't get out till two. Most of the other kids would be excused after a while or they'd go outside, but I had to stay for the whole service. After all the hymns and the scripture were over, the minister would preach, and once he got started . . . I don't know how the man lasted, how he had a voice when he finished. Well, the last piece we always did was 'Blessed Be the Tie That Binds,' and on this partic- ular Sunday when two o'clock came I was so exasperated—

I mean being kept there so long, three hours, just a kid nine or ten years old—that I played it as fast as I could. I can still hear how fast I played it. And Reverend Harrison looked at me and he said, 'Play it again and play it right.'"

• • •

Dunedin is a pleasant town on the Gulf of Mexico, just north of Clearwater, and its relatively few blacks—roughly one hundred and fifty—live in an area that covers only half a dozen blocks. Until 1915 there was no school in Dunedin for black children and there was no school bus system; black parents had to take their children to Clearwater. That changed with the arrival of a Quaker woman from Pennsylvania named Almira Chase. Finding the situation intolerable, she built a school which was called the Washington School and Social Center. Mrs. Chase was part of a long tradition of Quakers who went throughout the South in the decades after the Civil War building schools for black children.

"It was a little red schoolhouse, two stories high," Mitchell recalls. "It had a kitchen and a library, and it was just beautiful. There were only two classrooms and probably no more than twenty kids in each class. By the time I went there, Mrs. Chase had died and Pinellas County had taken over the school. The two teachers were Mr. and Mrs. Whitehead, who were black and who came out of the school system. Mrs. Whitehead was my first teacher. She could play the piano and also improvise a little, and she took an interest in me right from the start. She taught me simple chords and how to read a musical line—the equivalent of a lead sheet—and that gave me the fundamentals of picking out a melody and putting in my own chords. Every morning in school we had 'devotion,' and she made me play for that. We had this book called *Songs We Like to Sing,* and I still remember them—songs like 'Drink to Me Only with Thine Eyes.' One day Mrs. Whitehead played 'Trees.' It started off in D, and D was such a pretty key, and nobody ever played in D. She said, 'I want you to learn this,' and I watched her and then I played it, and that was the first time I ever played in D. I still play it the same way today. Sometimes she'd also let me play little jazz things—when we had some kind of program and the kids would get up and do their little dances. Those programs gave me my first chance to express myself at the piano because Mrs. Whitehead never played that kind of music. She always said, 'Oh, you play that.'"

But to grow up in a small black neighborhood in a small Southern town was to be isolated from almost all the newer sounds of music. A boy who wanted to hear such sounds would have to be lucky—lucky in the fragments he might hear on the radio or on a record, or in the people who might come to town and show him what he needed to know. For Mitchell the first such messenger was the jukebox in a neighborhood place called Dewey's Dew Drop Inn, which was owned by Mr. Dewey Davis. "The music on those records was awful—I couldn't stand it even then," Mitchell recalls. "But there was one number that all the kids went wild about. It was 'Tuxedo Junction,' played by Erskine Hawkins' band, a very good black band. The chord structure was very much like today's jazz voicings, and it was the first time I heard a sound that approached something I had been listening for. It pulled together what I wanted to say on the piano. Everybody who played the piano in our town played out of books that used the major triads for chords. If they played a C-major chord it was C-E-G, and that was that. But I hated that sound. Even then I never played those major chords, and to this day, unless Beethoven says C-E-G, I can't touch it."

For a Baptist church pianist to avoid the C-major triad and still not add any decadent notes would seem to be impossible. What *did* Mitchell play if he wouldn't play C-E-G? "I played C-G!" he says. "If you take that E out you're playing a fifth, which sounds O.K." Presumably W. A. Harrison's ear was sharp enough to detect the Devil's handiwork—a note that had been added—but not to hear one that had been subtracted.

"The first record that really blew my mind when I heard it on Dewey's jukebox," Mitchell says, "was Nat King Cole's 'Straighten Up and Fly Right.' It was smooth, and the man played fantastic chords. That kind of voicing I could really relate to. I'd go home to my piano and try to imitate what he was doing. Sometimes I could find it and sometimes I couldn't. But I noticed that if I played one of his chords along with chords of my own that didn't have those same voicings, it didn't feel comfortable. I instinctively knew there had to be some kind of unity. But I didn't know where the other chords were. And there was nobody around to tell me."

Into this vacuum, one day, came a black man named William Anderson. He lived in St. Petersburg and worked for Pinellas County, which sent him all over the county to teach music to black children and to find musical talent in black communities.

"We called him Mr. Bill," Mitchell says. "He had this old Buick that he drove from town to town, five days a week, and he came to us twice a month—on Wednesday afternoon at three o'clock, just when school let out. He'd ask the kids to show him what they could do, and he quickly found out who had talent. A lot of boys and girls in those black communities were very good singers, and they never would have developed their talent if it hadn't been for him. My cousin Alma Vaughan was one—he encouraged her and brought her music and taught her semiclassical songs that she had never heard before. Mr. Bill could play or teach anything, but he never took children beyond their interests. He'd go with whatever he found in each town. He had a little choir here and a little band there. In our town nobody had any instruments; I was the only kid who played."

The Methodists let Anderson hold his lessons in their church because it was right next to the school. "I just couldn't wait for three o'clock," Mitchell says. "The other kids would fade away pretty soon, but I'd just sit there at his left and watch him play. He had fantastic hands that could play these great tenths that I didn't know were possible because my own hands were small. We became very, very close. The man was a fabulous technician. He could get over the keyboard like I had never seen anybody. He could get through the cracks—just go all the way between the black and white keys. He played very much like Fats Waller, and his harmonies were much more sophisticated than any I had known. He played the first major seventh I ever heard. Mr. Bill was the first visual contact I made with somebody's hands playing that kind of chord. Up to then I didn't have any idea what those chords looked like. Now I could put my *eyes* on them, and I'd stop him and say, 'How do you do that?'"

Chords weren't the only revelation; there were matters of dynamics and shading that had never occurred to Mitchell, who assumed that all piano pieces were played in the same plodding way. "Mr. Bill would make things happen to a piece," Mitchell says. "He always caught what it was that made a song interesting. He gave the whole composition more meaning by altering its rhythm or its volume. He was also a true improviser, so he could give a new dimension to what was already there. That was the first time I realized that a pianist could bring part of himself to what somebody else had written."

Mr. Bill knew his student well. "He never gave me an exercise," Mitchell recalls. "He just said, 'In time—it will come in time. Don't worry.' Because he could see my frustration. He could feel it. He was a man that hardly ever smiled. I remember his eyes were always so serious and he'd look at me and he'd say, 'Everything's going to be all right. I'll always be here.' I knew nothing about the history of the man. He never talked about himself. He must have been in his late forties at that time, and I'm sure he had been on the road someplace. He was a great big man—he looked like a black Santa Claus without the beard—and he was immaculate. He was neat to the *teeth*. He was fat and he had a big stomach and he had this very serious fat face. Most fat faces look like they want to smile all the time. His didn't. But there was a very beautiful sound in his voice and also great affection. His voice was saying, 'You can trust me.' You felt that about him.

"Mr. Bill must have come for two and a half or maybe three years. He came at a time when I really needed him. I needed his strength. My parents had been divorced the year before and I was going through all this turmoil with my father and this feeling that I was all alone. I clung to him much more than I did to my father because I was so afraid of my father. Mr. Bill unlocked a lot.

"One Wednesday afternoon Mr. Bill didn't come, and he never came again. I never did find out what happened to him. He just dropped out of my life."

• • •

The void that William Anderson filled was so deep and painful that Mitchell can only begin to talk about it now. One day the fabric of his life was intact; the next day it wasn't. Despite the arguments with his mother over what to practice on the piano, he knew she was bringing him up on values that were different from those of the other neighborhood kids. "Even the eating habits were different," he recalls. "Everyone else was having biscuits and bacon and I was having shredded wheat."

Lilla Mitchell got her sense of possibility, growing up in Reddick, Florida, from her own father. "He had never been to school at all—his background was all slaves," Mitchell says, "but he insisted that his daughter get an education. Reddick didn't have a high school—it was just farmland around there—so he sent her to a boarding school called Fessden Academy. My mother told me how her father got up every day at 2 A.M. and walked twelve miles to a job in a lime mill— and twelve miles back—to earn enough money to send her to this school. After that my mother went to Edward Waters College in Jacksonville. She was a very good singer of classical music and she apparently had fairly decent teachers. But when she got out of college there was just absolutely no place for her to go except church. So her life was spent training other singers: anyone she could find who had any talent at all."

What it was that caused her to relinquish her son, when he was only eight, Mitchell never knew and has never asked. But he remembers the day with photographic clarity. "I had on a white linen suit," he says. "My mother always used to dress me so nicely, and I thought that was great. And my father tied my ties—I always wore a tie—and I used to wear pongee shirts. I still don't know what pongee is, but that's what I wore, and I guess the shirts didn't cost much because an old lady down the street made them for me. Well, I had on this white linen suit, with short white pants, and white socks, and shoes, and we were in this judge's office. I didn't understand what was going on, but I do remember that the judge's name was Judge Byrd. How I remember that man's name I don't know. Judge Byrd said to my mother and father, 'You have a very talented son and what are you-all thinking about him?' As a kid I was known among the white people because they used to come to our programs in church and at the school. 'Don't you think you should be thinking about this boy?' he said. 'I'm going to take him with me and I want you-all to sit down here and talk, and when I come back, whatever decision you-all have made, that will be it.' And he took me by the hand and we walked off and he bought me a soda and talked to me. But I was very nervous. Then we came back and the divorce was final and I was told I was going to live with my father and see my mother in the summers."

That was the end of the pongee shirts and all the other graces. "Everything changed," Mitchell says. "I never did make the adjustment; I don't suppose I've gotten over it yet. When my mother left I felt a great emptiness because all the affection and care that she gave me were no longer there. My father was just not that kind of person, and of course he couldn't take the place of my mother anyway. I played the piano a great deal then to try to escape the pain—or, possibly, to play about it. I would make up things and they all turned out to be very sad sounds. I was left alone most nights and I was very afraid of the dark. My father was still a fairly young man and he went out a lot."

Ivory Mitchell, Sr., also changed his sights after the divorce. He went to night school and learned the builder's trade; later he became a contractor and built many houses in the Dunedin area. The love that he gave his son primarily took the form of food. "He'd fix my breakfast and then go to work," Mitchell recalls. "Then he'd come home and fix me lunch, and at night he'd come home and fix me dinner, and then he'd get dressed and go out. In many ways he was a good man. With all his worries he kept his feet on the ground—he knew exactly where he wanted to go. But he was very hard on me. I had to be in the house by 6 P.M., and in Florida in the summer it didn't get dark till nine-thirty, and everybody else was out. And he'd say, 'Don't hang with that person,' and 'Don't talk with this one.' How could you help it? The whole community was about three blocks long and three blocks wide. Anytime you said anything too loud the whole neighborhood could hear you."

. . .

The Baptist religion, which might have been a solace, was just the opposite. "The most terrifying part was that this man W. A. Harrison would preach about how everyone would be damned and go to hell," Mitchell says, "and his strength would go up and up and these poor people would be screaming and crying. I sat at that piano for years and listened to people cry. They were uneducated people who had eight children and had to slave all week, and then they'd come to church on Sunday and they'd be more terrified than when they came. It was unbearable; I can't stand to see people cry.

But I had to play because I was the only one who never made any mistakes. Not that my piano playing was that good, but all these other ladies hit a lot of wrong notes. They'd make little runs that started in the key of C and ended in the key of God knows what. So I was stuck.

"What I learned very early was that this religion was not for me and that I had to find some other outlet. Music became my religion. When I played certain things on the piano at home I was totally out into something else. I cried and became very emotional and I thought, 'This must be what they mean, all those people at church and all those great feelings. This must be what the minister means when he talks about the spirit.' But I never felt any of that in the Baptist church or cried over what I played there."

Salvation, promised by the Baptists, came instead from the Methodists. Mitchell began playing for their Sunday evening service when he was about ten. "It was just a joy," he says. "The Methodist order of service had all these beautiful little cadences that knocked me out, like 'Glory Be to the Father.' I loved those major chords that entered into a minor sound, or those minor sounds that entered into a major sound. I loved to find nice harmonies for those passages. The choir always had a couple of numbers, and I could really stretch out on those and do anything I wanted to. Most of the numbers were gospel songs. I still remember one called 'I'll Fly Away'—'when this life is over, I'll fly away.' It was like a jazz song; it had a sort of blues quality, and I played it with a slight syncopation, which you could *never* do in the Baptist church. With the Baptists you stay right on the beat; the rhythm is only implied.

"Those gospel songs in the Methodist church stirred very deep feelings. When the people sang I could feel the vibrations. Even though they weren't musicians they had something that they wanted to express in music. It was the first time I had an emotional contact in church with what they called religion. I loved knowing that I could help the choir and enhance their singing. As long as I stayed within the structure of the piece, I was allowed to improvise around it. The name of the lady who directed the choir was Mrs. Marie J. Hart, and I'll always bless her because she said, 'Play as you wish.' That was my freedom."

The Methodist church paid Mitchell three dollars a month—the first money he made as a pianist. He was never paid by the Baptists in all his years of servitude. "You were a member of the church and that was your job and you did it out of gratitude," Mitchell explains. With the Methodists he so enjoyed playing that he hardly thought about the money. One day he realized that he hadn't been paid for six months and he mentioned it to Mrs. Hart. She told him to go straight to the minister and tell him. He did, and the minister said they had been giving the money to one of the church trustees, Stan Hooks. "Mr. Hooks was a very, very proper man," Mitchell says, "and he told the minister he had been giving the money to my father. So that night I went home and said, 'Dad, Mr. Hooks says he's been giving you my three dollars a month and I haven't been paid for six months.' My father said, 'He hasn't given me one penny.' He was so mad you could see him turn blue—my father was a very black man—and he turned almost purple. He walked out the door and said he'd be right back. I don't know what he said to Mr. Hooks, but he came back and he said to me, 'You are not to play for the Methodist church ever again.' I was crushed—because that was the only outlet I had, and here it was just wiped away."

• • •

"In those years my father hollered at me so much," Mitchell says, "that at one point I went deaf. It was psychosomatic. There was a fantastic doctor in Dunedin that I went to when I was a kid: Dr. Meese. He built a hospital in Dunedin that's named for him and he lived upstairs and had a beautiful grand piano up there. He was always interested in my playing, and when I went to his office he'd ask me if I wanted to go up and play the piano. Doc Meese understood a lot of things about me that most people didn't. When I was small he'd sit and take me in his arms and ask me if my father had been hollering at me. I remember once he told my father, 'This boy's extremely nervous,' and another time he said to him, 'If you don't change, this boy may have a nervous breakdown.' But my father continued to scream and yell at me, and I was always shaking, and one day I just went totally deaf, so he could scream all he wanted and I couldn't hear him. I couldn't hear anything! I can remember playing the piano and not being able to hear what I was playing. The kids used to be very cruel—they'd come up right behind me and yell in my ear and I couldn't hear them. This went on for about eight months."

Mitchell credits Dr. Meese and several other white people in the community for helping him to survive those years and encouraging him about his future. "There was a woman named Mrs. Skinner who took a great interest in me," he says. "The first time I ever saw a Steinway piano was in her house. I used to mow her lawn, and when I was finished she'd ask me to come in and play her piano. That was the first time I ever knew what an in-tune piano sounded like. As a child I had much more support from white people than I did from my own community. The black people just took what I did for granted. They thought, 'That's Ivory, Jr.—he plays the piano.' Which is fine. But the white people had heard much more music and they naturally had a broader appreciation of it. They understood its possibilities for me."

One summer, when Mitchell was eleven, the urge to get away overwhelmed him. At that time he had a job mowing the lawn for a number of families and was getting paid fifteen cents an hour. "It was really nothing," he says, "but it was enough so you'd make eight or ten dollars a week, and I had saved my money. I couldn't think of anything but getting away from my father. I went to the station and bought a ticket to New York on this train called the *Silver Meteor*. I was so excited that I had to show it to all the kids; none of them had ever been out of the state, and neither had I. Well, one of the children—her name was Geneva—told her mother,

'Ivory, Jr.'s going to New York this summer,' and her mother said, 'Oh, is that a fact?' Later this lady passed my father on the street and she said, 'I think it's such a nice thing for you to send your son to New York.' My father said, 'I know nothing about this.' 'Well,' the lady told him, 'Geneva says he has his ticket.'

"My father didn't say anything to me. So finally I went to him and said, 'Dad, may I go to New York? Or to New Jersey?' I knew that my father's sister, who loved me very much, lived in Trenton, so I said, 'Can I go to see Aunt Bert?' And he said, 'You take that ticket and you go back down to the station and cash it in because you're not going anywhere. You did not consult me.' But by now I was thinking very quickly and I said, 'Can I go see my mother in Jacksonville?' Because I knew that the train to Jacksonville keeps going to New York. And he said, 'Yes, you can go see your mother, but you cash in that ticket to New York.' So I said I would.

"The day came for me to leave, and I got on that train, and when that train got to Jacksonville it kept going and I was on it. I went right on to New York. But what I didn't know was that my father was going to Trenton that same night; he didn't tell me. I left Dunedin on a Friday morning at eleven-twelve and got to New York on Saturday because I took an express. My father left on a train at 10 P.M., but it was a local, so he didn't get to Trenton until Sunday.

"Well, my train got into Pennsylvania Station at ten in the morning and I spent the whole day in New York. I walked all around the Thirty-fourth Street area, as far as the Empire

State Building, just having a fantastic time, eating hot dogs and junk like that. Then in the evening I got on the train and went to Trenton to stay with my aunt. When I got there she said, 'I'm not expecting you until tomorrow, and anyway I didn't think it was you—I thought it was your dad.' I said, 'What do you mean?' She said, 'I got a telegram from Ivory Mitchell saying he was arriving Sunday afternoon, and we're going to meet the train.' Well, in Trenton the train platforms are below street level and you can look down on them from a sort of catwalk. When the train came in at one o'clock I looked down and saw this coat and knew it was my dad. I panicked: I ran right out of the railroad station. My aunt must have said something to my father because she knew I was scared to death. I stayed out till five, and when I walked in my father was sitting there and I said, 'Hey, Daddy,' and he said, 'Hi.' That was the end of it. I never heard anything more. The next day I got on the train and went back to Florida."

. . .

Musically he was returning to barren terrain. Mr. Bill Anderson had come and gone, and the sounds that Mitchell's ear craved were not in the air. They weren't even on the radio. Historically, radio has been the servant of popular music, bringing the big bands and small combos and brilliant soloists through the night from clubs in New York and Chicago. For boys and girls who had an ear for music, the sounds that came through the radio were tantalizing: maybe, someday, *they* could make those sounds. But how? What combination of notes and instruments produced harmonies so smooth and rhythms so captivating? To listen was to begin to learn.

But not in Florida. "To this day," Mitchell says, "the music on Florida radio is sort of retiring. It's like piped-in music— a lot of violins. When I was a boy I almost never heard anything on the radio that was original or good. We had one program that would play requests, and that was *The Sun Dial,* which came on from St. Petersburg every morning before we went to school. I used to tune in because I was so desperate, but nine out of ten songs were bad. We also used to get station WLW in Cincinnati. Don't ask me how Cincinnati got to Dunedin. But Cincinnati is just not on the track of music—on the radio it's mostly country and bluegrass."

Only one beacon pierced the Floridian gloom, and that was Duke Ellington. "I'm quite sure Ellington was the first black band that had a national radio show," Mitchell recalls. "Every Saturday afternoon I'd come home about three or four and I'd wait by this old RCA Victor radio we had. It was a half-hour show, and we were never so impressed. I remember somebody saying that Ellington was making seven hundred dollars a minute, and we thought that was fabulous. There are two things I remember about Saturday afternoons. One was the voice of that man who broadcast the Metropolitan Opera—was it Milton Cross?—and the other was Ellington. I loved that program.

"But Duke Ellington's voicings were not the kind you could go to the piano and put your fingers down on. The clarinet jammed next to something else. G and A flat together in the same chord. To me those close-together voicings were just not to be believed. If you listened you could tell that all the voices related to each other, but you couldn't put your hand on how to do it. And even if you happened to hit the same notes on the piano, you couldn't make that same sound because of the way it had been orchestrated for the clarinets and the baritone saxophones. I never asked Mr. Bill about those Ellington harmonies because he was totally into Fats Waller, and I was also so impressed with *that* sound and trying to learn how to play it. But Ellington was probably the biggest outside influence on me."

. . .

Mitchell outgrew the red schoolhouse, but he remembers it as an important place in his life. In fact, its recent history—as I found when I visited Dunedin to see the neighborhood myself—perpetuates what Mrs. Chase had in mind back in 1915. Under the name of the Chase Memorial it continued to be the public school for Dunedin's black children until 1964, when Florida schools were integrated. The red schoolhouse closed—but not for long. Across the street, in the Shiloh Baptist Church, where Mitchell had been the indentured pianist, a woman named Lureen Leland had just launched a project called the Dunedin Educational Enrichment Program (DEEP) to help black children who couldn't read or who had other learning problems. She and her five teachers, all volunteers, held the program in the community room of the Baptist church, which was too small to contain the children who wanted to be taught—and the noise that they made.

"Everyone was going crazy," Mrs. Leland says. Noticing that a bona fide schoolhouse was now vacant, she petitioned Pinellas County to let her operate DEEP in the Chase Memorial. The county leased it to her for one dollar a year. "They charged me a dollar that first year," she says, "and never sent me another bill." For the next thirteen years Mrs. Leland and her teachers built DEEP into such a helpful program that in 1978 it was brought into the county's school system. Today the little red schoolhouse is no longer red; it's white, and it's closed, but it still has a big wooden sign that says "CHASE MEMORIAL."

By contrast, Pinellas High School, where Mitchell went next, has receded in his memory. The school had no orchestra, but it did have a chorus that he accompanied, and he also played every day for the assembly. "I played for them to march in and I played whatever they sang," Mitchell says, "but that's really all I remember." Like his Sunday chore at the Baptist church, performed year after year under the unrelenting watch of W. A. Harrison, it was work that was expected of him.

One member of the staff, however, did stretch him as nobody had before. "Her name was Vivian Henry, and she was an English teacher in the high school," Mitchell says. "In fact, she's still there and she's still one of my favorite ladies. She played the piano very well, even though she wasn't the music teacher, and she was by far the most educated musician I had ever met. She did a wonderful thing for me. She made me write down the stories of all the composers and the operas, and I still have all those old notebooks today. She said, 'You won't understand why I'm making you do this now, but you will later.' I became fascinated with who all these people were that I'd never heard of—Bach and Mozart and Chopin—and what their music sounded like. But there were no records; I would read about Chopin and how his fingers flew across the keys, but I never heard a Chopin étude. I took piano lessons from Mrs. Henry for about a year, and she gave me a lot. But that was one of the hardest times of my life. I was more and more bitter toward my father and hurt by the divorce, and my attention span was so short that I couldn't retain anything. Mrs. Henry would have been such a good teacher for me, too."

In his later high school years Mitchell had several chances to get out of Dunedin. "Doc Meese was the first person to talk about my going away to study music," he recalls. "He said to my father, 'Why don't you let this boy leave here and go to Juilliard?' And I think he would have paid for it. But my father wouldn't hear of it. There was also a white lady who came to our house three or four times to talk to my father. I can't remember who she was, but she must have been something in music. She wanted me to go away with her to study in upstate New York, and I would have been delighted to go. But my father just flatly refused."

The problem of moving on was abruptly solved in the spring of 1946, when Mitchell was seventeen and finishing high school. "One of the guys I was going to school with—Alroy Butler—said, 'Man, let's volunteer and go into the service.' And I said, 'O.K., let's do it,' not knowing whether we'd be taken, or even giving it much thought. So a bunch of us got on our bicycles and went down to the recruiting center, and sure enough we got our papers and we were off into the army. I was never so glad to get away. I thought, 'I'll never come back here again—never!' That decision shaped my whole life. Because it was when I got in the army that my musical education really began. And of course that was also where I met Ruff."

3 . . . Muscle Shoals

Willie Henry Ruff, Jr., was born on September 1, 1931, in Sheffield, Alabama, and part of him has been there ever since. Many of his relatives still live in the area, and he still goes back regularly—whenever he isn't teaching at Yale. He stays in a simple house that he built on an acre of nearby farmland he used to plow when he was a boy: his roots in the community are deep. But in his many years of going back he never went as a performer. His career took him all over America and all over the world, but not to his home town. The right occasion never came along. Then, in the winter of 1982, it did, and I asked if I could join him. I wanted him to show me the places where he grew up and to tell me who his teachers were and what kinds of music he heard.

Sheffield and its twin town of Florence are in the northwestern corner of Alabama, almost in Tennessee. They are separated by the Tennessee River. Like many American towns on opposite sides of a river, they developed opposite personalities: Florence sedate and conservative, Sheffield raffish and easygoing. But the river was also a unifying force. Well into this century it gave the area—which is collectively known as Muscle Shoals—a certain renown, bringing from both directions a steady traffic of jazz musicians and riverboat bands and minstrel shows. The two towns were also on a direct route of two railroads, the Southern and the Louisville & Nashville, that were favored by itinerant entertainers because there was no need to change trains and possibly get lost. In any case, jazzmen who played Memphis and Nashville and Birmingham could hardly help passing through Muscle Shoals in one way or another, and they enjoyed stopping off there—the atmosphere was always friendly and Prohibition never prohibitive. The area even had an authentic patron saint, W. C. Handy. The "father of the blues" was born in a log cabin in Florence, and nobody seemed to mind that his most famous blues had St. Louis and not Florence in its title.

But after the boom years of World War II, much of the life drained out of Florence and Sheffield. The defense plants shut down; television became the nation's nightly entertainment, and any musicians who were still touring America played the big cities and got there by plane. Muscle Shoals was no longer on the circuit. One person who was saddened by this trend was Willie Ruff. He felt that the area's younger generation had lost contact with a musical heritage that had enriched his own life, and he rallied a group of local citizens to do something about it. His idea was that Florence should have an annual W. C. Handy Music Festival, which would attract the best musicians every summer. Seed money to launch the festival would be raised by a benefit concert that the Mitchell-Ruff Duo would give; the concert in turn would

be publicized by a week of events saluting the musical glories of northwestern Alabama.

The week of February 15, 1982, was duly chosen, and a
citizens' committee went to work with gusto. When I arrived
in Florence near the end of that week, the festivities were in
full momentum. The newspapers were full of celebratory ar-
ticles, and I was delighted to read that Saturday had been
designated "Willie Ruff Day." I've never known anyone else
who had himself a day. I caught up with Ruff in the auditorium of the Coffee High School, where he was giving a talk
to the students, most of whom were white. Ruff was nattily
dressed and was obviously the local boy who had gone North
and made good. But there was none of this in his manner.
His talk never touched on the glamorous world to which he
had escaped; he spoke entirely about the place that had nour-
ished him and given him his start.

One of the things he told the students about was the
time when Henry Ford came for a visit and the region almost hit it big. There is a mile-long dam just east of the two
towns, at a bend in the Tennessee River where the water
drops one hundred feet, and in 1921 Ford inspected the site
to see if electric power could be harnessed cheaply. He was
so impressed that he talked of moving his factories to the
Muscle Shoals area and turning it into a "little Detroit." An
age of prosperity seemed imminent, and speculators laid out
plots that were connected by roads with names like Detroit
Street and Michigan Boulevard. Then Ford decided not to
come, and the land was planted over. "So if you go out there

today," Ruff told the students, "that's the only place in America where you'll see cotton fields that have curbs."

Growing up in Sheffield, Ruff said, was a musical treat. "The whole area was heavily peppered and spiced with music — mostly religious music and jazz. For instance, there were always a lot of chitlin struts. A chitlin strut is like a rent party: people held them to raise money. They'd serve chitlins and coleslaw and bootleg liquor. The bands that played there didn't get paid; they just played for what they could eat and drink. A good chitlin strut was always 'seeded' with dance teams. My mother was an extraordinary dancer, and she was in great demand at these events to loosen people up. The idea was that if people have a good time they'll stay and dance and eat and drink and it will be a profitable evening."

Ruff said he got his own musical start at the age of three, taking advantage of a pure singing voice that people seemed to like—or, at any rate, couldn't avoid. "I was too small to cross the street by myself," he said, "so I'd get a neighbor to put me across one street and then I'd make my way to across from Mr. McNab's grocery store, and from there I'd call to Mr. McNab to 'bring me to sing.' He'd come and bring me to the store and I'd sing 'There's an Old Spinning Wheel in the Parlor' and 'St. Louis Blues.' I'd earn all the candy I could eat."

But Ruff's first important influence was a white boy named "Mutt" McCord. "We lived in an integrated part of Sheffield," Ruff recalled. "All the families on our side of the street were black and on the other side they were all white.

Mutt lived directly across the street from us. He started playing the drums and getting interested in music when he was
sixteen and I was seven. He was the same age as one of my
older brothers, George Fred, and they were very close friends.
In fact, when my brother died three years ago, Mutt was a
pallbearer. They'd never seen that in the Baptist church here—
a white pallbearer at a black funeral.

"Mutt had the first electric phonograph I'd ever seen,
and he would set it out on the grass in front of his house and
put on a Gene Krupa record and play it as loud as he could.
Then he'd set up his own full set of drums and try to follow
Krupa. Or he'd put a Count Basie record on and try to follow Jo Jones. Or he'd put on a Duke Ellington record and
try to follow Sonny Greer. He'd get this transfixed look on
his face; he'd go into another world—he just wasn't from
around here. And I worried him until he taught me how to
do it. He took me under his wing like a big brother during
all those years and taught me everything he knew about drumming and music and rhythm. First he gave me a snare drum,
and then he gave me a cymbal, and he taught me how to read
music, and he insisted that I learn how to do it correctly or
not at all, or he wasn't going to fool with me. Mutt and I
had—and still have—an unusual relationship for people of
different races, not just in the South but anywhere, because
what we shared was an inside view of listening to people play
drums and understanding what went into it. Any drummer
who came to town, we'd take off together and hear him.
Mutt got so he could imitate the great drummers who came

with the minstrel shows or the ones who played in the Sanctified church here—anything he heard. I never knew anybody who could pick up so many different styles. He's got red hair and freckles and blue eyes, but he's as African as anyone you ever met."

Ruff said he wanted more than anything to be a drummer. But the more he studied with Mutt, the more he was overwhelmed by the immensity of the task. "To be a master drummer you had to know so much more than just the drums. You had to know all about music and how to put it together and make a total musical statement. I realized that I could never know that without having more experience than I could possibly imagine. I knew I'd have to give up the drums and learn about music in some other way."

• • •

When Ruff finished talking to the students and chatting with some who came up later to ask questions, he said he wanted to drive me over to Sheffield. First we drove through Florence, past the log cabin where W. C. Handy was born, which is now a museum. Ruff had told the high school students about Handy's long life and his rich accomplishments as a musician. Though Handy is best known for composing "St. Louis Blues" and other standards, Ruff has always admired him most for a task he undertook when he was quite old: making four-part vocal transcriptions of sixty Negro spirituals. They were spirituals that Handy had heard as a boy in the Greater St. Paul's Methodist church, which his minister father had founded. Handy was afraid that the spirituals would die if they weren't preserved in some form, and he wrote out the four parts exactly as he remembered his elders singing them.

Just how beautiful these arrangements were—and how difficult—Ruff had only discovered within the past month. He had scheduled as the opening event of the week-long festivities a Sunday afternoon concert by a black choir singing the spirituals in Handy's father's church. Ruff himself would rehearse and lead the choir. Two problems arose, however, that he hadn't foreseen. One was a shortage of bass voices. The choir consisted mainly of women, and their training was in gospel music, which has only three parts; it doesn't have a bass. Only two men could be found with voices deep enough to sing the bass parts, and one was in his seventies and quite weak. Ruff responded to the crisis, as usual, by improvising. He recruited a tuba player to supplement the two men, surmising that the tuba would be a good match for the human voice at that register and would provide just the right volume.

The other problem was that Handy's arrangements were a tough nut for the gospel singers to crack. Not having heard the spirituals when they were young, they had to learn the music by reading it; somewhere, between generations, an oral tradition had been snapped. The choir went at the material doggedly in three weeks of arduous rehearsals and still only mastered three spirituals: "Stand on the Rock," "Give Me Jesus" and "Standing on the Sea of Glass." Still, the concert was a huge success. People came from all over the county—far more than could fit into the church—and they overflowed into the basement and other rooms that were rigged with loudspeakers. Ruff compensated for the brevity of the musical program by giving a brief talk explaining Handy's feat of preservation. Then, when the choir had finished singing each spiritual, he got the congregation to join in and sing it again. Fervor ran high.

Now Ruff drove me down the wide main street of Florence—a typical Southern town with the usual facade of banks and stores—and over the bridge to Sheffield. Just crossing the Tennessee River seemed to lighten his spirit. "The intensity of the Bible Belt was always much stronger in Florence than it was in Sheffield," he recalled. "They used to say about the two towns, 'The drys have their laws and the wets have their liquor.' Sheffield was where the *low-life* people lived." Ruff spoke the word with relish, meaning it to embrace all the occupations that lubricate the day. "My mother sold liquor at home," he said. "If any of my sisters were to hear me admit that my mother was a bootlegger they'd want to scald me. But it doesn't bother me. My mother had eight children to support, with no husband around, and she made five dollars a week working as a maid for a white family down the street. Still, she provided for all of us, whatever way she had to do it, without hurting anybody."

As the youngest member of the family, Ruff was often the only one left at home to sell his mother's private stock to people who might develop a midday thirst, and he learned to count and make change by the time he was three or four. "We had many steady customers," Ruff recalls. "The icemen were regulars because they made their deliveries all day long. They liked Mama, and it didn't hurt that I had good-looking sisters, so it was always a very polite transaction." The icemen instructed Ruff in such niceties as how to flush liquor down the toilet when a visit from the law seemed imminent, instead of down the sink, where it would be trapped in the curve of the pipes and found by the cops, who always brought plumbers' wrenches. One neighborhood defense against sudden invasion was an ordinance forbidding the police to enter a house if anyone inside was disrobed; they could be accused of lascivious carriage. "Miss Bethalina was famous for that," Ruff said. "Anytime they knocked on her door she'd call out, 'I ain't decent.'"

Reading was another skill that Ruff learned early. His sisters taught him so that he could go to first grade when he was five and they wouldn't have to stay home with him. "I learned to read aloud," Ruff said, "and I wasn't timid about standing up in front of people—I never have been. When the folks at the Sanctified church found out I could read they gave me a Sunday school class. I was five years old and some of my students were almost a hundred. They had been born in slavery—anyone who was ninety in 1935 was born long before the Civil War—and most of them couldn't read or write. I'd read very simple things like 'God is love' and they'd make a big fuss over that. They thought I was a scholar."

Ruff drove me to the neighborhood where all these

childhood talents had been imparted. Sheffield is a town of tree-shaded streets and comfortable-looking frame houses. I had the sense of a community that was compact and congenial. Ruff's boyhood house, however, has been torn down to make room for some senior citizens' housing units. We walked around what was once Ruff's front yard. "My two biggest musical influences were right here within earshot," he said. "One of them, of course, was Mutt McCord. That's Mutt's house right over there across the street. The other one was the Sanctified church. The music of the Sanctified church was as influential on me as any music I ever heard, and the person who influenced me most was Miss Nance, who was their drummer. That church is gone now, but it used to be right behind our house. I mean it was literally in our back yard.

"There's no denomination as loud as the Sanctified church. Any instrument that anybody wants to bring to the service is welcome: drums, tambourines, bells, brasses. During revival times we'd get these traveling troupes of Sanctified musicians. Powerful trombone players would arrive from Memphis, which was the home of the Sanctified religion, and you could hear them for blocks. Our neighbors used to say, 'Those Sanctified people must think God is deaf.' Folks came from all over Sheffield—both white and black—to listen to the music and watch those services. It was just people doing Africanisms in their religion. They danced to the drum and they'd become possessed by spirits and lose awareness and shout in unknown languages and do things that just weren't acceptable in other Protestant churches. At that time being African-like wasn't a thing that was admired, and some of the visitors laughed at those people. But I never did because I loved the music. Sometimes the prayer meeting on Wednesday night went late and the whole neighborhood would drift off to sleep letting that music just wash over them."

I asked Ruff to tell me about Miss Nance. "She was an older lady who was a farmer," he said. "She never had any education and she couldn't read or write. She had a pigmentation disfigurement that's not uncommon among black people, and her skin was blotchy and unattractive. But there was something otherworldly and angelic about her when she played the drum. It was a big bass drum, the kind they have in a marching band. She played it with a wooden spoon that had a heavy sock tied around one end. She played both ends of the spoon—the end with the sock and the end that was plain wood—so she'd get a contrast of a thump and a slap. She got more music out of that drum than anyone I ever heard. She could get many different tones out of it. In fact, it sounded like several drums, not just one, because in addition to using the stick with her right hand she'd hit the other side of the drum with her left hand—with the hand itself. She could play rolls and she could play tremolos. She could make the drum say 'Ay-y-y-y-y-y-*men!*' and she could make it say 'Ha-a-a-a-le-*lu*-jah!' And she'd be mouthing the words at the same time—that helped her if she was playing a response to the sermon. In the Sanctified church a good drummer or piano player will work the preacher, just the way a good pianist in a silent movie house will work the film, and nobody ever worked a preacher like Miss Nance.

"I took piano lessons from a woman like that. Her name was Miss Winston and she was the organist in the First Baptist Church here in Sheffield that our family attended, which was in a black neighborhood known as Baptist Bottom. There wasn't any organ, but people who played the keyboard in church were always called the organist; they were even listed that way on the program. Miss Winston knew exactly how to lead Reverend Yarborough through his sermon. She knew when to cool him off and she knew when to heat him up. She knew what kind of chords to play when he started talking about how he remembers the morning his mother died, and when he hears his mother's last words she had special licks for that. When Miss Winston thought the sermon was winding down she'd start playing a long drawn-out cadence until finally the minister got tired, and then at the natural place she'd give a signal to the choir, and the choir would come up singing. Oh, it was high drama!"

I asked Ruff what became of the piano lessons. He said they were fifty-cent lessons that his grandmother bought him because she hoped he would grow up to play piano in the Baptist church. That dream collapsed, Ruff recalled, the year he went to mourners' bench. "During revival time the Baptists go looking for converts," Ruff explained, "and the candidates for salvation come to church and sit on the mourners' bench, where they mourn for their sins and ask the Lord to deliver them. You can go at any age—whenever you can promise the church you're ready for salvation. I went when I was about nine, after I'd started playing the drums with Mutt. You sit there in the evening and get preached at—they admonish you about all the things you should do to get saved—and during the day you're supposed to just think about the Lord. Well, one day I was out in the yard doing that, and I was making up some songs, and my grandmother came out of the house preaching like a funeral. She said, 'Why, you sinful rascal! How do you expect to go to heaven whistling and humming those dirty blues?' I told her blues weren't anywhere on my mind—I was just making up a song. That was what I was offering. She said, 'I don't want to hear you singing that Devil's music.' So I didn't stay on the mourners' bench very long. I think preaching ran me away from church, because that never was the attraction. Whenever I was moved it was always by the music."

• • •

Music was literally in the air during Ruff's boyhood, brought by boat and by train. Stern-wheelers going up and down the Tennessee River would put in at Sheffield to unload passengers and cargo, and many of them had calliopes out on the deck. "You'd hear them coming a couple of miles away because the sound carried across the water," Ruff recalled. "I'd hear that calliope and I'd run down to the river. The boats would leave off some freight and take on wood for fuel and maybe pick up some cotton, and while they were there at dockside the calliope player would give a free concert. Those men were great players. They wore red-and-white-striped shirts and sleeve garters, and when they played the calliope these big clouds of steam would billow up over their heads and evaporate. People standing on the dock would marvel at that. They'd say, 'Watch that booger play till it rains on him.'"

Minstrel shows also came to Sheffield regularly. They would set up their tent in a field several blocks from Ruff's house, and he and Mutt McCord would hurry over to hear the drummers, whom they greatly admired. I was surprised to learn that minstrel shows traveled through the South; I had always thought they were offensive to blacks because they consisted of white actors doing black acts in blackface. Ruff explained their somewhat circular history. They started in the time of slavery, he said, as an entertainment on plantations: blacks making fun of whites. "What you'd see was slaves strutting around in tails and high hats, imitating how the white folks acted in the big house, and that was genuinely funny. Later these acts were seen as such a vibrant theatrical form that they were adapted to the commercial stage, and at that point became whites imitating blacks who were imitating whites. Some of the white entertainers were very funny, and they also were good actors and dancers and mimics. Those were the minstrel shows that eventually made their way up North and that made people like Jolson famous with his Mammy songs.

"Meanwhile, in the South, minstrel shows branched off into still another form. The performers were blacks, but they no longer imitated whites. They did comedy routines on black subjects—the kind that Pigmeat Markham became famous for—and they played a circuit of black vaudeville houses that sprang up throughout the South. The acts were booked by an organization called the Theater Owners Booking Association, or TOBA, which got to be known in the trade as 'tough on black asses.' Many great musicians like Fats Waller were part of those traveling minstrel shows, and forty years later when I had them up to Yale they still remembered coming through our town. Pigmeat Markham said, 'Man, are you from *Muscle* Shoals?' He remembered being there in 1928. Some black minstrel shows also made their way North because the North was so heavily populated by Southerners. Theaters like the Apollo in Harlem would book them, especially if they featured gospel quartets or rhythm-and-blues singers that the Southern blacks missed. But down here they always played in tents. And the town where they put up their tents was always Sheffield, because that's where the action was."

One other external influence was records. When Ruff was about ten he began plowing, near the neighboring town of Killen, for a family that one of his sisters had married into. "My brother-in-law's mother, Mrs. Hardin, owned all these records," Ruff said. "She'd buy every new blues record that came out—and as soon as I got home from the fields she and I would put those records on an old wind-up Victrola. The needle had to be changed about every four records—I remember they came in dime packets—and I'd keep up with the needles and just play the records over and over while she cooked. I didn't know who I was listening to; later I realized that I'd been listening to men like Lester Young and Jo Jones. There was one record with a saxophone sound that was one of my favorite records of all time. I grew up with it. It was called 'Evening,' and it had Lester Young on the sax and a vocal by Jimmy Rushing. Some other songs of that period were 'Cow-Cow Boogie' and 'One O'Clock Jump' and 'The Honey Dripper' and 'Tuxedo Junction,' and all of Count Basie. But radio wasn't an influence on me at all. I never listened to the radio because we never had electricity."

Ruff himself hadn't yet learned any instrument except the drums, and opportunities to play were sparse. The black school in Sheffield, which ran from kindergarten through twelfth grade, didn't have a band because no equipment was provided by the board of education, as it was in white schools. Instead, the state sent a black teacher from town to town to try to get black children interested in music. Every three weeks he came to Sheffield, where he tried to start a band. "I was the only kid in the school who had his own instrument and knew how to read music," Ruff said. "It was a pitiful beginning—this man played the piccolo, and I played the drum, and there was a dentist's son who had a cornet."

It was common in the South at that time for black schools to be given hand-me-down equipment that the white schools no longer wanted—old footballs, for instance, and old books —but not old instruments. Ruff took a certain strength from the inequities. "There were marvelous ways that people invented to overcome in style," he said. "In fact, I know a lot of people who credit that disadvantage for their being able to make themselves better than they otherwise would have been. We had a brilliant black doctor in Sheffield named Dr. Long. He was one of the most inspirational men I've ever known and also one of the most tragic. He was frustrated because he wasn't given hospital privileges and many other rights that he had earned. But he had no patience with kids in Sheffield who complained about having to study out of books that had the backs torn off. He said, 'If there's not a page missing out of it, it's not a secondhand book. It's got as much learning with the back off as it has with the back on. Of *course* it's an injustice. But you can waste your time complaining about it, or you can get what's in it.'"

What finally made a difference in Sheffield was World War II. "The war touched our lives in ways that are hard to understand even now," Ruff says. "Suddenly there was great prosperity—everybody's parents had a good job, or a better job than they'd had before. Musical instruments finally began to materialize. But before our little school band could get to be anything, my mother died and I had to move away." Ruff was sent to Evansville, Indiana, to stay with his father, whom he hardly knew. Less than a year later he happened to meet a cousin who had gone into the army and who told him about such appealing aspects of army life as regular meals and the possibility of playing in the band. Ruff faked his age and his father's signature on a parental consent form and became a fourteen-year-old soldier. In another year he would meet a soldier named Dwike Mitchell who would teach him to play the bass. But if he was beginning to think about any instrument besides the drums, it was one of the horns.

I asked Ruff where that idea came from. I assumed that it was the memory of those powerful trombonists who came from Memphis to play in the Sanctified church. Or the memory of those evenings out in Killen listening to Lester Young's saxophone on Mrs. Hardin's Victrola.

"The thing that gave me the notion of playing the horn," Ruff said, "was the sound of a great contralto in our Baptist church named Miss Celia Appleton. She had that rich, horn-like quality in her voice. When people used to ask me how I decided to play the French horn I said that it was the closest I could get to Miss Celia. Or to Mr. Buddy Jenkins, who sang bass in the church choir. They both sang a lot of solos, and people in the church were just overwhelmed by the extraordinary quality of those two voices. It wasn't only the beauty of the voice; it was the poetic expressiveness. It was what they could bring to a melody. I can't ever remember a funeral in Sheffield when people didn't have it in their will that they wanted Miss Celia or Mr. Buddy to sing. That's a sound that I'll never forget. It's more distinctive in my ear than Louis Armstrong."

• • •

After Ruff and I had walked around his old neighborhood we got back in his car. He had tickets to the Mitchell-Ruff concert that he wanted to give to various friends and relatives. (Ruff was once married, incidentally, and has a twenty-five-year-old daughter, Michele.) As it turned out, some of the friends and relatives seemed to have no interest in the tickets and almost no grasp of the event he was inviting them to attend. He was just Willie Ruff. If he had a career somewhere else, that was his business. For now he appeared to be someone who had never left small-town Alabama. I was delighted by the down-home cadences that had crept into his speech, by idioms and regionalisms that were as old as the black South. It wasn't the first time I had been struck by Ruff's gifts of adaptation. I had heard him charm foundation executives in Manhattan and conservatory students in Shanghai—both in their native language. His remarkable ear was one of the agencies of his survival and his success.

We stopped at one house to drop off three tickets with Ruff's stepbrother, an old man named Buddy-Boy Pruitt, who had been a truckdriver for the TVA but was now retired —seemingly to a chair out in the yard, in which he sat as motionless as a cat. Ruff told Buddy-Boy that the tickets were for him and his daughter, Ann, and her husband, Bubba, who also lived there. "When that piano picker starts to play," Ruff said, "they're going to have to strap 'em to the seats." I had never heard Mitchell (or anyone else) called a piano picker, but the term had a vitality that conveyed Ruff's admiration for Mitchell. Buddy-Boy didn't trouble himself over exactly what was going to happen on Sunday night; all that really mattered was the transaction of giving and receiving the tickets. As we got back into the car Buddy-Boy said he'd wait and see what Ann and Bubba were planning to do. If they came, he would probably come too. That, Ruff explained to me, was a certainty: Buddy-Boy can't stand to be alone after dark.

Next we dropped off a pair of tickets with a white man of about seventy-five named James Kirsch, who owns an auto body shop and, by virtue of that fact, is Ruff's most unusual music student. Ruff's car is a 1948 Packard that he coveted for four years as it sat rusting in a weed field outside the Muscle Shoals Recording Studio. Next to Nashville the studio is the most popular one with the brightest stars of rock, gospel and country-and-western music, and many of them come there to make records; thus Muscle Shoals is again a magnet for musicians. The sound engineer who owned the Packard was too busy to fix it, and he finally sold it to Ruff in 1979 for three hundred dollars—by far the smallest of the sums that would go into its revival. Ruff had the engine rebuilt and then faced the task of restoring the dilapidated body and interior. He took his problem to Mr. Kirsch, who said he was too old to do the work himself but that he would teach Ruff how and would let him keep the car in his shop. Ruff would pay in money for the parts and the paint; but for the instruction and the space Mr. Kirsch wanted a different kind of payment.

"I knew that Mr. Kirsch was a great admirer of a honky-tonk sax player named Boots Randolph, out of Nashville," Ruff told me. "But one night—just before I went to see him about the car—he was watching a religious television program and he heard a saxophonist playing 'The Lord's Prayer.' Mr. Kirsch said it was so beautiful that the preacher congratulated the sax player and told him that old Gabriel was going to have to move over. Mr. Kirsch said to me, 'If I could play that song like that feller played it on TV, just one time in church before I died, I'd *have* to be let into heaven.' Hearing that song reminded him that he had a saxophone down in his basement—he had bought it thirty years before for his son, who didn't take to it. It was a wreck. But I knew I had to teach Mr. Kirsch that song if I wanted to get my car restored."

Ruff can teach anybody anything, but this was one of his knottiest challenges, for, as he soon found out, Mr. Kirsch had little aptitude for music. "And 'The Lord's Prayer' happens to be an unusually difficult piece—it rambles all over the place," Ruff said. His only hope would be to devise a special system of notation. He made a chart consisting of X's and O's to correspond to the words and to Mr. Kirsch's fingers—an X meant that he should keep the finger down, an O that he should lift it up—and the odd-looking document was tacked to Mr. Kirsch's wall. Luckily for Ruff, the tricky climactic measures of "The Lord's Prayer" continued to give Mr. Kirsch trouble. "He got the first part O.K.," Ruff said, "and told me he hoped to have the whole thing memorized soon. That had me worried. I thought, 'He's almost up to Amen and we haven't even started spray painting.'"

Mr. Kirsch came out of his house and greeted Ruff warmly. He was a short, bald man with a fringe of white hair. Around his neck he was wearing the leather strap that saxophonists wear to hold their instrument and that some of the great ones wear habitually as a badge of their art.

"How are you coming on 'The Lord's Prayer,' Mr. Kirsch?" Ruff asked him.

"Pretty good, Willie," he said. "I'm up to 'Forgive us our trespasses,' but I still can't get 'For thine is the kingdom.'" Ruff reassured him that all those high notes would be hard for anybody, but Mr. Kirsch was obviously disappointed. He said he thought he had the whole piece memorized and only last week had persuaded his wife to let him play it for her Wednesday afternoon ladies' group. Evidently this was no small act of persuasion—his wife, an organist, had exiled him to the basement for his practice sessions. Ruff had told me that Mr. Kirsch was both very nervous as a student and very proud of his new skill. "Anybody who comes into the body shop with a torn fender, Mr. Kirsch gets his sax and plays as much of 'The Lord's Prayer' as he can remember."

I asked Mr. Kirsch how it had gone on Wednesday afternoon. "I started off fine," he said, "right up through 'Hallowed be Thy name.' But then I froze. I think it was at 'Thy will be done.' Or maybe I got up to 'Give us this day.' Anyway it wasn't very far. I couldn't go on. Finally I just had to turn around and walk out of the room."

Ruff told him he had made charts for two more songs that use similar fingering—"My Country 'Tis of Thee" and "You Are My Sunshine"—and Mr. Kirsch brightened at this news of fresh territory to conquer. Mrs. Kirsch came out of the house and Ruff asked if they needed more than two tickets to Sunday night's concert. They said that two was just right and that they were looking forward to it. Mrs. Kirsch gave Ruff a curious look.

"Jimmy," she said to her husband, "I don't know how that feller can get you to put the right finger on those keys."

...

On Saturday morning Mitchell arrived, and he and Ruff put in two days of giving informal jazz demonstrations for children and for the citizens who had organized the week's events. Sunday night brought the long-awaited concert. It was held in the large and handsome auditorium of the University of North Alabama, whose campus is in Florence. Some of the patrons were worried that the turnout would be small, despite all the publicity, and that this would jeopardize the W. C. Handy Music Festival. But one look at the people flocking into the auditorium put those fears to rest. It was a big crowd and a happy one.

I saw many faces that were familiar: students from the high school in Florence where Ruff had talked, friends from his old neighborhood in Sheffield. I saw Buddy-Boy and Ann and Bubba. I saw Mr. Kirsch—nicely dressed and wearing his saxophone strap—and Mrs. Kirsch. In the front row I saw a sandy-haired man of about sixty who was conspicuous for his pleasure at being there. I asked someone who it was and learned that it was Mutt McCord. It hadn't occurred to me that Ruff's first teacher might still be around. I introduced myself to him.

"This is the thrill of a lifetime for me," Mutt said. He had brought his two granddaughters, Christy and Melanie, and he introduced them to me. I asked him for his early memories of Ruff. "You know, I just can't imagine a more wonderful friendship than that boy and I had," he said. "Bill Henry was a skinny little kid with red hair, and he always had manners. That's how his mother brought him up. During the war when I went into the service he was very good to my mama and daddy. He'd come over every day and ask if they needed any wood cut, or anything else done, and he wouldn't ever take any money for it.

"That boy loved music. After I took up drumming I got a big bass drum that I played in the high school band, and Bill Henry thought that was the prettiest thing in the world — it was like a Christmas tree to him. When I walked to school for band practice he'd walk beside me beating that drum, and his eyes would just sparkle and shine. Blacks weren't allowed on the football field of the white high school, so while we practiced he'd sit at the edge of the cotton patch next to the field and wait till band practice was over, and then he'd walk back home with me, beating that big drum."

I asked Mutt whether he had kept up with his own drumming. He said that when he came home after World War II he became a builder and a construction superintendent, but that he continued to be a part-time drummer, sitting in with bands that accompanied many Grand Ole Opry singers and other soloists who gave community concerts at the National Guard armory in Sheffield. In 1968, however, a head-on car crash almost killed him and broke so many bones, including his wrists and his right foot, that doctors told him he wouldn't walk again. He did walk again, but his drumming days were over. To take the place that drumming had filled in his life, he became a professional dog trainer and is now the contented proprietor of Mutt's School of Canine Control. He has kept in touch with Ruff not only as a friend but as a builder. When Ruff built his house out in Killen, on the land he had once plowed, it was Mutt who taught him how and helped him to build it.

The concert began. Ruff made a brief homecoming speech that thanked the people for their attendance, which had raised the money necessary to proceed with the W. C. Handy festival in August. (It was duly held, with Dizzy Gillespie as its principal star.) Ruff was unabashedly proud to be on that particular stage on that particular night. Mitchell struck the first few chords of "The More I See You"—chords of unusual elegance—and was off in high gear. Usually it takes him a while to achieve the emotional breakthrough that at some point in every Mitchell-Ruff concert lifts it to a high plane of excitement. This time excitement was in the air from the beginning.

Afterward, people from all of Ruff's old and new constituencies came backstage to see him. One of them was Buddy-Boy.

"Willie Henry," he said when he got to Ruff, "I never did know what you does for a living. But you sure does it."

4 ... Columbus

For a few years right after World War II, Lockbourne Air Force Base, near Columbus, Ohio, was like no other military facility. It was a constellation of gifted black men and women who had been brought together by events that could only have occurred at that moment in American life. The events were set in motion soon after Pearl Harbor, when thousands of black men tried to enlist for flight training in the armed services and were all rejected. The premise was that blacks couldn't learn to fly.

But as aerial combat in Europe and the Pacific depleted the supply of white airmen, the army changed its mind about the learning ability of blacks and accepted them for pilot training. This still left the question of where they would be trained. An integrated base was unthinkable—white soldiers wouldn't put up with that. The solution was to establish a training unit at Tuskegee Institute, the famous black college in Alabama, and there the most qualified black men were assembled and taught. If they needed a vote of confidence in that early period they got it one day when Eleanor Roosevelt visited the base and asked a black flight instructor to take her up. Watching her vanish into the sky, the official who had escorted her from Washington said to the other member of the White House party, "Lord, don't you tell the President what she's doing."

The blacks turned out to be superb pilots, and the combat record that they compiled with the 99th Fighter Pursuit Squadron, under Colonel B. O. Davis, Jr., escorting Eighth Air Force bombers on raids deep into Germany, was one of conspicuous gallantry. When the war in Europe drew to an end, in April of 1945, the much-decorated pilots were brought home and assigned to Freeman Field, Indiana. There they were subjected to the same Jim Crow discrimination that had prevailed before the war. They were classified as "trainees," barred from white officers' clubs and relegated to an inferior club of their own.

Protesting this treatment, sixty black officers forced their way into the white officers' club and demanded to be court-martialed. Their wish was granted, and by the end of the week, as many other black pilots joined the protest, refusing to sign an agreement not to use facilities designated "for whites only," 101 of the returning heroes had been arrested and confined. In the resulting wave of bad publicity the War Department realized that to keep 101 war heroes under arrest was hardly the way to defuse the crisis. A more creative response would have to be found, and it was. Lockbourne was converted into an elite base for all the black specialists who couldn't be integrated at that time with white air force units: not only the pilots of the 99th, but black lawyers, for instance, and doctors and engineers and musicians. B. O.

Davis, Jr., the son of a black general himself, was made base commander.

"That base had the highest number of college degrees per capita of any military installation in the United States," Ruff says, recalling what he found—besides Mitchell—when he got to Lockbourne. "Of course those pilots of the 99th had already been handpicked for training at Tuskegee. And their wives were even better educated. Most of them wanted to be schoolteachers, and they had gone to college and graduate school while their husbands were overseas. So anybody who was at Lockbourne knew he was there because he had something special to offer."

Every black musician wanted to be sent to Lockbourne because of its band. "To get into that band was a mark of distinction," Ruff says, "not just because it was a great performing group but because it had the reputation of a conservatory. It was the creation of one man—a legendary bandmaster named John Brice. He only had the rank of warrant officer, but he was a highly educated man—he had taught military history at Howard University—and he was a personal friend of President Roosevelt and of all the top generals. He knew the birthday of George Marshall's wife and Mark Clark's wife and every other general's wife, and when these dates came along he'd call Washington and get someone to send a plane for the band. Omar Bradley was his buddy. He knew that Bradley's wife liked the overture to the *Poet and Peasant,* and he'd show up with a band of 160 and play it for one of her teas.

"He was a tall, thin man who was very impressive as a conductor. He had all these great airs. He'd wave his arms like Toscanini and he could screw up his face to look as if he was in ecstasy. B. O. Davis hated his guts because Mr. Brice never asked for anything in the right way." (Warrant officers were called "Mr." in the army at that time.) "He'd call FDR or Mark Clark, and in the middle of the night Colonel Davis would get a phone call about something that he would have been perfectly glad to do if Mr. Brice had just gone through channels. But Mr. Brice wasn't going to fool around with young'uns. He'd been in the army longer than this boy had been *living*."

The fact that Mr. Brice had 160 musicians is the surest proof of his political skills. "He was only supposed to have twenty-eight men, like anybody else," Ruff says. "That's the normal strength of a military band. But if he heard about a good musician anywhere in the air corps he'd call the Pentagon and that man would be transferred to Lockbourne." Mr. Brice also assembled all the old musicians he had ever soldiered with—men who had gone through World War I and had stayed in the army and made a career as musicians. "It was a very small guild of men," Ruff says, "but they were all wonderful musicians and teachers, and Mr. Brice knew just how to use their skills. That's what made Lockbourne a conservatory."

. . .

Dwike Mitchell was at Lockbourne long before Ruff

got there. But even before that—during his basic training in San Antonio—his musical education had begun. "I met a soldier there named Early Scott who was an old guitarist and arranger," Mitchell recalls. "He really sort of fell in love with me as a musician and decided he wanted to teach me everything he knew. He found this little house at the edge of the base that had a piano, and every night after dinner we'd go over there and play and he'd explain all kinds of things that I had never known or even thought about. Then he started a little band and I was in it. Of course I didn't know anything. I had never seen that many saxophones. In Dunedin there were no saxophones—who played the saxophone? So that was where I first learned about other jazz instruments, and how music was arranged for them, and how to play with them as a pianist. I accompanied everybody in that band, and I loved it because I listened to all those great things that those musicians were doing, and I was so in awe of what I heard that it just had to rub off on me. When basic training ended we were all put on a train, including Early Scott, and were sent to Lockbourne field, outside Columbus. And there I met the most fantastic musicians in the world."

Mitchell was assigned to the band, even though there are no pianos in a military band. "I guess Mr. Brice felt that I had some kind of talent and he kept me," Mitchell says. His debut, however, was one that he remembers for nonmusical reasons. "Mr. Brice told me, 'I want you to march with the band, so you've got to play the glockenspiel.' I hadn't ever played one of those things, and the keyboard is sideways, so

I had to walk with my head twisted like a contortionist to see where the keys were. One day all these generals came from Washington and we were supposed to play for them. The parade ground at Lockbourne was surrounded by deep ditches on all four sides—you had to cross a little bridge to reach it—and the ditches were full of water because it had been raining a lot. When the generals were ready Mr. Brice said, 'Come on, boys, let's go,' and the band started playing and we began to march. In that band the glockenspiel marched first, and next came the conductor, and after him came the band. Now another thing about the glockenspiel is that it's very loud. After playing it for a while, if somebody had said to me, 'There's a fire on your back,' I wouldn't have heard it because I was just totally deaf from hitting those chimes. Well, somebody gave a command to turn, and I didn't hear it, and the glockenspiel and I just kept going straight and slid down into the ditch and disappeared. The generals broke up, they thought it was so funny. It was the low point of my musical career. But the good part was that Mr. Brice never sent me out again. He just didn't use the glockenspiel anymore. So I thought, 'The spirits were so kind to let me disappear in that gully.'"

Another exemption was in the area of "P.T.," or physical training—a duty that few enlisted men have ever managed to avoid. "One day Colonel Davis announced that everybody had to take P.T.," Mitchell recalls, "and that included the band, which he said would have no special privileges. Mr. Brice said, 'O.K.,' and then he got on the phone and called Washington and said, 'General, this P.T. is for the birds and I'm not having my boys go out and do this terrible stuff, and I'm going to have to fight this,' and the general said, 'O.K., Brice, O.K.,' and he called Colonel Davis and said, 'No P.T. for the band.' Poor Colonel Davis—he was powerless with this one warrant officer."

Fortunately for Mitchell, Mr. Brice's empire didn't begin and end with a military band. Deploying his 160 musicians according to their talents, he also formed a concert band and two jazz bands, and it was into the concert band that Mitchell, his glockenspiel career over, was thrown next.

"I knew an older man named Sergeant Proctor," Mitchell says, "who was a marvelous conductor, but he was also a man who understood people and their problems. He was like a psychiatrist, and he would just nurse you through. He became a very, very close friend. Sergeant Proctor suggested that I learn the Grieg A-Minor Concerto and play it with the concert band. I had never even *seen* a concerto. I was still a slow reader of music, and this concerto was the most frustrating thing—it was just too full of notes. But Sergeant Proctor said, 'You can do it,' and he worked with me at night. It went so slowly that many times I cried. I just couldn't get it.

"There was a captain named Alvin Downing who was a wonderful pianist, and one day I saw him walking on the base and I told him I was having all sorts of problems with the concerto. One thing about Lockbourne was that everybody knew everybody else and it didn't have a rigid military feeling. You could speak to a captain; maybe you saluted and maybe you didn't. Captain Downing said, 'Listen, bring the piece to me and I'll work with you.' Alvin pulled it together for me as a pianist. He played the parts very slowly that I had struggled with, and if he played it slowly enough the notes finally came together and I could hear what they were supposed to sound like. He also showed me how to work out the fingering to these difficult parts, because I had never had any training for that kind of music. In fact, I was still trying to play everything with my thumb and my first three fingers because that had been the easiest way for me when I was a child.

"Well, I learned it. And after that I rehearsed it every day with the band for I don't know how long. And then came the performance. I was never so scared in my life. I don't know how I got through it—every muscle in my arms ached because finally I just forced it. But I played it to the end; all those people who had worked with me were there, and I couldn't let them down. Can you imagine a boy coming into the army from Dunedin with no musical education at all and somebody saying 'Play this concerto'? It wasn't good, but I must have had guts to even try it.

"What Alvin did opened up a great deal. He helped me not only with things I had to play for the concert band— piano solos that Mr. Brice wanted in the middle of a longer semiclassical piece—but also with the jazz band. We had two jazz bands, and fortunately I was with the number one band, because that's where all the arrangers were. They were fabulous arrangers. Arthur Wiggins was one of the finest—he still is—and he'd write fantastic things. And there was 'Tech' Jones, who was a Shostakovich freak. Everything he arranged was voiced like Shostakovich."

But it was another Russian who influenced Mitchell most. "One day a pilot came to our barracks," he says, "and told someone that he wanted to see the private who had played the Grieg Piano Concerto. I went out and here was this captain I had never seen before. He introduced himself and said I should call him 'Flaps.' That was his nickname—he got it after something went wrong with the flaps on his plane. He put me in his car and drove me over to the officers' quarters and sat me down in his room and put on a record of Rachmaninoff. The man was totally mad about Rachmaninoff. He had every recording of everything that Rachmaninoff ever composed—nothing by anybody else."

"Well, he played that first Rachmaninoff record and I began to cry. I couldn't believe that anyone had written music like that. The chords are so amazing—they go through incredible progressions, and they're also very jazz-oriented. Of course it was the first classical piano I'd ever heard. You can't imagine what it was like to have been down in Florida all those years and listened to nothing—because all we ever got on the radio was the opera on Saturday afternoon, and that was singing. So when Flaps started playing these Rachmaninoff concertos for me I flipped out, and from then on he couldn't get me out of his room. Every day I'd call him and say, 'Listen, what are you doing this evening? Can I come over?' And he'd never say no. Flaps and I would sit in total silence and not speak a word and play concerto after concerto. We never played any other composer; when we got to the end we just started over. This went on for a year and a half. And then one day Flaps cracked up his plane and was killed. Today I often play the Second and the Third Concertos on the piano myself, and I always think of Flaps because he just sort of felt something about Rachmaninoff and me. That was the first big shake-up in my musical life."

There was only one other shake-up of the same magnitude, and it happened in much the same way, with an older mentor—in this case, Wiggins—bringing Mitchell a record of a pianist he had never heard before. The pianist was Art Tatum. "When he put that record on," Mitchell says, "I thought, 'This is absolutely impossible. How does one even attempt to do something like this?' Tatum seemed to have developed an intricate technique in order to baffle the listener—his tempos went all out, they went in any direction—and at the same time he kept this simple melodic line going. I was into Rachmaninoff by that time and I heard the same sounds in many of the things Tatum was doing.

"But then I thought, 'If it's impossible for Tatum and he's doing it, then it's also going to be impossible for me.' That's when I first started to think about touch. Because I realized that these people were getting sounds out of the piano that I had never heard before. They made the piano sound different—it lit up; it did something else. Tatum's top line would stand up so beautifully without being hammered, the way I'd always heard pianos hammered by people around home. So this was just total touch. And I began to teach my-self that: by listening to a sound and trying to duplicate it on the piano. If you listen very hard to a sound, every time you put your hand on the keys and don't get it you know something's wrong. But then one day you *do* get it."

Mitchell's real school, however, was the jazz band. "In theory Sergeant Proctor was in charge of it," he says, "but nobody was really in charge—it was just a very disciplined and dedicated group of people. I've never seen anything like it. There were eighteen men in that band—five saxophones, five trumpets, four trombones, guitar, bass, drums and piano—and besides being great instrumentalists those men wrote all our arrangements. We almost never played any stock stuff. All of them had distinctive styles, and each arranger would say, 'You have to play it this way,' which was the best possible training, even if you didn't like that particular style, because you didn't get locked into one way of playing. Wiggins' arrangements were absolutely beautiful, and they were also technically perfect—everything always fitted exactly, just like you put on your shoes. I'd love to hear those arrange-ments today, because I'm sure they're just as good now as they were then.

"But what I remember most was that those men were eager to show you whatever you asked about, and at that time I just had a thirst. I was totally immersed in nothing but this learning process. That was when I really became in-terested in music. That was when it hit me: 'This is what I want to do.'"

. . .

Meanwhile, at another base, Willie Ruff was taking his first steps into the world of music. Behind him was his basic training at a camp in Alabama and a six-month hitch at Camp Stoneman, a port of embarkation in California, where he waited to be shipped overseas. Instead he was sent to Fort Francis E. Warren, in Cheyenne, Wyoming, to be trained as a truck driver. He was fifteen years old—just a skinny kid, he says, too small to be driving an army truck.

"One afternoon not long after I got there I was at the piano in the dayroom playing 'Pine Tops Boogie,'" Ruff recalls, "when the first sergeant came in and said, 'You ought to be in the band—we've got enough truckdrivers.' I was sent to the bandleader, a warrant officer named Mr. Ruffin, who gave me an audition on the drums. I wasn't very good, but he took me in because they were short. I had only been doing that for three weeks when the bottom fell out. A band that had been at Fort Lee, Virginia, was broken up and about twenty of its musicians were sent to our camp. And in this group were drummers the likes of which I had never heard.

"Most of the new musicians were cavalry sergeants who had been in the army for forty years and were near retirement. They had a considerable musical education. They had learned composition and orchestration and arranging, and they were inspiring because they had gone into the service to escape the strictures of civilian life and they had made music their career and taught each other. They were very elegant old men. They wore old-style military clothes—the uniforms were tailored, and the brass was right, and their shoes were well taken care of. They looked like college professors. Many of them wouldn't talk English. They had learned French and German and Italian overseas, and as a mark of their elitism they spoke those languages among themselves and wouldn't deign to talk to younger soldiers. There were some that I never *did* hear speak English."

With this influx the band was suddenly up to strength, and its instruments were a revelation to Ruff. "I'd never seen an oboe or a bassoon," he says, "I'd never seen the bass fiddle played with a bow. I *had* seen a baritone horn, but I had no idea how beautiful it was. These men made it soar. The baritone horn is the king of all brass instruments—the poet. Baritone-horn solos have the pathos that the cello has for the symphony orchestra, and the men who play it are the prima donnas of the military band. As for the drummers who came from Fort Lee, they were fabulous—both as jazz drummers and as percussionists playing classical concert music. It was clear that I was outclassed, and Mr. Ruffin said, 'Well, son, we really don't need you now.' He said I'd have to go back to the truck company.

"I've never been so miserable in my life—to see all these accomplished men, and the only way you could get to be like them was to get *old*. I was devastated by having to leave the band, and the next day I went back to Mr. Ruffin—I'm sure I had tears in my eyes—and told him that I knew I couldn't make it as a drummer but that there were still some weak spots in the band, especially the French horns. He was always fussing at them—they were always cracking notes. 'If you let me learn the French horn,' I said, 'I promise you I'll work hard and I'll be as good as those guys you've got very soon.' Actually what those guys played was the mellophone, which is sometimes called the peckhorn because when they play marches the only thing they play is *peck-a-peck-peck, peck-a-peck-peck.* Mr. Ruffin said, 'You want to be a peckhorn player?' I said, 'No sir, I want to be a *French*-horn player.' He said, 'There's nobody here who can teach you.' I said I had seen French horns in the supply room, along with instruction books, and that I'd like to check one out. 'Well, I'll think about it,' he said. 'But meanwhile you pack up your stuff.'"

Ruff packed his gear and then went to the supply room, where they gave him a French horn. The instruction book was in English on one side of the page and in German on the other. "It was written by a man named Oscar Franz," Ruff recalls, "and it was the most fascinating book I'd ever seen. I had only gone through ninth grade, and I used to read with my lips moving, but that book made playing the French horn sound like the most glorious privilege anybody could have. First it gave you the history of the horn, along with pictures, starting from when it looked like an animal's horn and going right up through rare old specimens in museums all over Germany. There was even a picture of a glass horn—someone had molded one in glass. And the book had all these florid illustrations of what the printed music looked like for Beethoven's Fifth Symphony, and the Brahms Third, and all that stuff, none of which I knew. Then it started right out teaching you how to play—except that it didn't give you the fingering. So I had to figure out my own fingering, and I never knew I was doing it wrong.

"I didn't start to be noticed by the older men until I began scuffling with that horn, and finally I asked a couple of them—knowing that older folks will always help you if you ask them—if they'd show me where to put my fingers. And this one great baritone-horn player named Pete Lewis, who was quite famous and who had been in the army thirty-eight years and was about to get out, started coming down to the boiler room where I did my practicing. He came down every morning after the first break in the band rehearsal to see how I was getting along and to help me through my scales. He really knew music. One day he said, 'The rest of those old boys are going into town to the beer garden tonight. You stay in the barracks with old Pete.' So we started practicing together in the evening, and he showed me how to find the right fingering, and I'd mark it in my instruction book and practice it all day down in the boiler room. I was coming along and I was starting to hear things."

After a while Ruff was allowed to sit in on the band's rehearsals, without his horn. One day the band was rehearsing a grandiose piece called "Ballet Egyptienne" that Mr. Ruffin was eager to play at a concert. The only snag was that it had a tricky horn solo that none of the horn players could get right—a failure that didn't go unnoticed by Ruff. "I asked

Pete Lewis if he could teach me how to play that Egyptian ballet," Ruff recalls, "and he said, 'Well, we can work on it, Junior.' So we worked on it at night and I worked on it during the day, and at rehearsals the horns kept screwing it up, and one day Mr. Ruffin said to me, 'You want to try it, Junior?' He was a very kind man—I think he had probably heard me practicing. So I went and got my horn and played the solo and pretended I was reading it; of course I had it memorized by then. And he said, 'All right, you are the first horn player,' and he put me in that chair and demoted all those other guys. And the next week I made private first class and a month later I made corporal.

"Pete Lewis kept on teaching me. He had classical records that he made me listen to—recordings of German orchestras that he had picked up during the war. He was my first important horn teacher. He said, 'Whenever you've got anything to play, always tell the story. You can tell the story with one note.' And he showed me how to tell the story with one note. He was known as 'Pete the Poet,' and I could see why. When he played that baritone horn it would move everybody to tears."

After several months the band was broken up and the strains of the "Ballet Egyptienne" were heard in Wyoming no more. Back East in Columbus, the event caught the attention of the one man whose ear was tuned to the sound of bands breaking up. Mr. Brice called Washington, and soon the best of the Wyoming musicians, including Mr. Ruffin, were at Lockbourne. Only a few old sergeants who were near retirement declined the honor, preferring to end their military days in peace and not under the tyrannical Brice.

Ruff had only five months left of his eighteen-month enlistment. He was sent to Oakland army base, where, severed from his French horn, he spent the rest of his hitch unloading transports returning from the Pacific. He remembers it as a grim period with only one bright moment: the re-release of *Fantasia*. "I went to the movies every night," he says, "and heard those French horn players and the Philadelphia Orchestra. And all that Stravinsky! We had been listening to a lot of Stravinsky in the dayroom back in Wyoming because Dizzy Gillespie and Charlie Parker and the other beboppers all wanted to sound like Stravinsky and were starting to play weird."

Discharged from the army at sixteen, Ruff went to New Haven to live with his sister, who was employed as a maid at Yale. Freedom, however, was no pleasure. Ruff wanted to get back to music and didn't have enough money to buy a horn. "I also missed the army a lot," he says. "Having been in during those formative years, there was just nothing about civilian life that was congenial." On his third day he got a job at the Yale School of Medicine, cleaning the cages of the animals that were used for research. His boss was a small Russian-Jewish man named Emil, who took an interest in Ruff and asked him about his time in the army. Hearing that Ruff had been a horn player, he became highly animated and began to whistle the themes of various symphonies and concertos, quizzing Ruff to see if he knew them. Emil turned out to be a lapsed musician himself; he had played in the Russian army band.

"I told him I really wanted to get in that band out in Columbus," Ruff says. "But I was nervous about it. I'd have to quit my job and pay my way out there. Emil kept after me about it. He said, 'Take a chance. What's to lose? Go talk to them.' So I took a bus to Columbus and went to Lockbourne. I got on the base because I was still wearing my uniform, and I found Mr. Ruffin. He said, 'Boy, I'm glad to see you—we need horn players.' I said, 'Do you think I can make it? I haven't touched a horn in months.'" Mr. Ruffin got a French horn and told Ruff to find a bunk and act as if he belonged there and to start practicing for an audition with Mr. Brice. Speed was important because Ruff would lose his corporal's rating if he didn't reenlist within thirty days.

"The audition wasn't great, but it got me in," Ruff says. "That had been part of my decision back in Wyoming. I told myself, 'I've gotten run off the drums, but next time I'm going to learn something that nobody's going to run me off,' because no band ever has enough horns. So I got in that famous band that I had heard so much about. And then they took me right over to headquarters and swore me in."

. . .

Mitchell remembers the new arrival well: "He was always like a little kid. He had all this hair, fire-engine red, practically down to his eyebrows, and he had a lot of energy—I guess we all did. At that time the band had a radio show that

I was supposed to do, and I needed a bass. Ruff came to me and said 'I want to play,' so I said I'd teach him. Sergeant Proctor had taught me all the positions because I wanted to see how it worked, and Ruff had a good instinct for the instrument from having been a drummer. So we started, and every time he made a mistake I made him go stand in the corner, and he hated that, and he'd scream and holler. He had the loudest scream you ever heard. But he never made that mistake again. He'd say, 'I'm not getting in that corner.'"

Ruff thinks his new teacher was unduly harsh—"he not only made me stand in the corner, he made me stand on one leg"—but he guesses that Mitchell needed to inflict on a younger victim the indignities that his elders kept visiting on him. Mitchell was the most unsoldierly of soldiers, nonchalant about the rules and amenities of military conduct. "Mr. Brice put him on all kinds of punishment," Ruff says. "He must have shoveled fifty tons of coal. But they all put up with him because he was such a bright spot as a soloist for us. He could elevate the currency of the band with his virtuoso performances. In fact, it was during one of these concerts that Lionel Hampton heard Mitchell and told him he wanted him to be his pianist.

"Mr. Brice needed Mitchell so he could take the band to Washington and outshine that official band down there. That band in Washington didn't play any concertos. Who ever heard of an army marching band playing a concerto? But we had arrangers who could take Rachmaninoff or Grieg or Tchaikovsky and reset it tastefully for the instruments that we had, and it came off sounding like the Philharmonic. Everyone at Lockbourne came to our concerts and took great pride in them. The children on the base grew up hearing classical music, and we all felt that we were part of a vibrant cultural community."

But it wasn't the concerts that made Lockbourne special. Ultimately, what Mr. Brice was running was a school. The day began with a rigorous two-and-a-half-hour rehearsal for the concert band. Then the band broke up into classes devoted to harmony, ear training, arranging, composition and other such subjects, which were taught, at Mr. Brice's insistence, by men like Proctor and Wiggins, who had had conservatory training themselves. This period might also be devoted to section rehearsals involving groups of brasses or winds. In the afternoon the band would practice marching, for it had become the show band of the air force, very much in demand, and it was constantly being flown to bases all over the country. Three or four DC-3s were needed to take the 160-man band and all its instruments on these far-flung gigs, but at Lockbourne there was no shortage of planes and pilots. In fact, the chief pilot was a legendary flier named Chappy James, who later became a general. Arriving at a base, the band would give a marching band performance on the drill field. Then, in the evening, it would give a classical concert in the base theater.

Ruff recalls his years with the Lockbourne band as an extraordinary education. His two main mentors were Sergeant Wiggins and Sergeant Proctor, especially Proctor, who played the baritone horn, the trombone and the bass. Ruff was rapidly learning the bass himself by playing jazz with Mitchell, and the two men quickly became close friends. He also started taking French-horn lessons every Saturday with the first horn player of the Columbus Symphony Orchestra, Abe Kniaz, who was then in his mid-twenties. "Mr. Brice encouraged any man who was musically ambitious to go beyond what was being crammed down his throat," Ruff says, "and we admired the men who went out of their way to get private lessons."

Lessons with Abe Kniaz were only incidentally lessons in music. "He began each session," Ruff says, "with all the reasons why I was embarking on a futile exercise—an attempt to find a professional career as French-horn player in a symphony orchestra. That just wasn't a possibility for blacks. As a young Jew he was tremendously preoccupied with the plight of the underdog, and every Saturday he went to great lengths to tell me what I was up against and to prepare me to make peace within myself.

"He found something in me that he could mold, and he took special care to teach me everything he thought I'd need to know. For well over a year he scheduled me as his last student on Saturday morning and I'd stay through dinner with him and his wife. He taught me how to speak and pronounce English properly. He taught me German. He told me what to read. He knew I was deficient in my education and he said, 'While you're working at the craft of playing the horn you've also got to get yourself ready to attend some institution of higher education.' It was Abe who urged me to go to Yale to study with Hindemith and who wrote my letter of recommendation. In fact, it was Abe Kniaz more than anyone else who prepared me for my career."

What Ruff remembers most about Lockbourne was an insistence on proficiency. Mr. Brice was a demon for self-improvement. "He kept emphasizing the rivalry for jobs that black musicians would face, both in the army and in the outside world," Ruff says. "The impression that he was always trying to make on youngsters was that we must never be trapped by the usual excuses that society uses to exclude blacks: that they can't read music; that they don't have the right symphonic tone; that they can't arrive on time; that they're careless about detail. What he couldn't stand was lack of interest in one's musical betterment, and any sign of laziness that he saw in his men he'd punish severely. If they didn't like it he'd ship them out."

Ruff stayed at Lockbourne for two years. In the second year Mr. Brice died of leukemia, and as his formidable power ebbed away the band was put to a different use. "A Colonel Getz came from Washington," Mitchell recalls, "and put together a big variety show called *Operation Happiness* that used all the talent at the base, including everyone in the band, and he also got some Wacs, so we had dancing girls, and we had singers and dancers and comedians, and we traveled by plane and played shows from one end of the country to the other. It was really a fun show—very well done and very professional. I was the pianist in the jazz band, which was one of the star features of the show. I trained a group called 'The Five Ivories' that came out and sang very modern harmony. Their special tune was 'Poinciana.'"

Mitchell's three-year enlistment ended when *Operation Happiness* was in San Francisco, and he left the show there. Discharged into civilian life, he used his G.I. Bill of Rights to start his formal musical education at the Philadelphia Musical Academy, losing track of Ruff completely. Ruff, discharged later when his own hitch was up, went back to New Haven and entered Yale. They were on their way.

"For me the army was everything," Mitchell says. "I had a lot of problems in the service, believe me, coming from the background I did, and those men became my family—Wiggins and Proctor, and a great drummer named Elvin Jones, and Henry Mitchell, who was an amazing saxophone player and a very fine man, and Harold Dyer, and Ruff. Except for Ruff they were all much older men, and I could go to any of them and they would take any amount of time. Sergeant Dyer would sit and talk to me until two o'clock in the morning—just talk me through my problems, which nobody had ever done before. And it seemed like they were happy to do it. In fact, I think we all really loved each other—it was just that close as a family. These men were also very educated men, and they took pleasure in passing on their knowledge of things they had read.

"That was my only introduction to life. When I was a child I felt that my father was trying to crush everything. He always seemed like he wanted to say, 'No, you can't do that.'

These men at Lockbourne were saying, 'Oh, there's nothing to that. Here, let me show you how it's done.' It was my saving grace."

5 . . . Davenport

Saturday, March 5, 1983

Mitchell and Ruff and I are on a small Mississippi Valley Airlines plane, lurching through a Midwestern winter night. We are bound for Davenport, Iowa, where the two men will spend five days as "visiting artists" in the Quad Cities—Davenport, Bettendorf, Moline and Rock Island—and in several surrounding communities. The schedule is heavy: it calls for them to give three public concerts at night and to give jazz demonstrations during the day in various elementary schools, high schools and colleges, on one television program and at the Rotary Club's Monday lunch.

What is on our minds right now—apart from the smallness of the plane—is whether Ruff's bass will arrive in time for the first concert, tomorrow afternoon. He and Mitchell are coming from a performance at the University of Alabama, in Tuscaloosa, and their plane connection at O'Hare Airport in Chicago, where I joined them, was a close one. The bass, which travels in a protective case that Ruff designed and that he once marketed for other bass players, has been checked through with the luggage and will have to be retrieved at the airport on Sunday. Ruff accepts this as a condition of the life that he and Mitchell have been leading for almost thirty years. Many of the campuses that they visit are in out-of-the-way places, and when they go from one engagement to another, hurrying through a big airport to catch a regional flight, they often get ahead of their bags.

Ruff begins to talk about the many black colleges where they have played in the South. He remembers not only their names (Bluefield, Fort Valley, LeMoyne, Morris Brown, North Carolina A & T, Tougaloo, Tuskegee) but their locations and their areas of excellence. "Livingstone College in Salisbury, North Carolina—that's a place with wonderful teachers," he says. "Talladega is probably the best black college in America; their graduates can go anywhere." But his memory of nonblack colleges is just as selective; when he names some of his favorites—Catawba, Principia, St. Cloud— I've never heard of any of them. I only know about the famous colleges where he and Mitchell have made an impact as teachers: Yale, of course, and Dartmouth and Duke, where they were artists in residence. Now I begin to realize how much of America's educational landscape they have touched.

"Last December," Mitchell tells me, "we did a concert at the University of Chicago, and we had a television session in another part of the city right afterward. It was a tight connection, so somebody hired a limousine to drive us to the TV station. The chauffeur was a nice-looking black man in a uniform, and he greeted us very warmly. He told us he could hardly believe he had the Mitchell-Ruff Duo in his car. He said he had heard us in a concert when he was an undergraduate at Dillard, which is a black college in Louisiana. I looked at this man's hair that was turning gray and I thought that was a *long* time ago. It must have been the late 1950s. He said that hearing us had changed his life—that it was his first encounter with a kind of music that has meant a great deal to him ever since. He said he's done well and is now the owner of the limousine service, but when he saw our names on the dispatcher's sheet he had to take that job himself. He gave us his card and told us if we ever need any help in Chicago he'll drive us anyplace we want to go."

Sunday

We're staying at the Blackhawk, a gloomy hotel in downtown Davenport that's named for the great Sauk chief. The Quad Cities are bunched together on the banks of the Mississippi River, which is unusually wide at this point. Two of them, Davenport and Bettendorf, are on the Iowa side; the other two, Moline and Rock Island, are on the Illinois side, and they are joined by three bridges that nobody would call modern. They have a combined population of 375,000 and regard themselves as "bustling." But they have a bypassed look. They are too big to be towns and too small to be major cities: they are not Chicago or St. Louis or Des Moines. The great river that was the reason for their existence no longer nourishes them, and even the legendary Rock Island Railroad has stopped running.

They also don't look like cities that get visited by many

artists. I suspect that Lois Jecklin, director of Visiting Artist Series, Inc., who met us last night, has worked miracles of persuasion to bring painters, sculptors, writers and musicians to Quad City schools and factories. These are no-nonsense cities—conservative and suspicious of frills. They are the Detroit of heavy farm equipment: John Deere, Caterpillar, Case and International Harvester all have major plants here. But the industry is depressed and unemployment is at twenty percent. In such a spare environment the arts would seem to be the ultimate frill.

Mitchell and Ruff's first concert is scheduled for two-thirty at Augustana College, across the river in Rock Island, and they come down to the hotel lobby to meet Lois Jecklin, who has found Ruff's bass and is ready to drive us there. The two musicians are wearing their tuxedos. Ruff is the one who decides how the Duo will dress, and I'm surprised that he has chosen to go formal for a Sunday afternoon in the Midwest. Augustana turns out to be a Lutheran college with a green-domed stone administration building of the kind that gives every American college of a certain age its character. The auditorium, however, could belong to any state university that expanded in the 1960s; it has sixteen hundred seats, and as Mitchell tests the piano I stare out over the vast and empty expanse. But husbands and wives and teenage boys and girls begin to trickle in—a family audience— and by two-thirty they have filled more than half of the hall. Probably very few of them know anything about the Mitchell-Ruff Duo, and now, when the two men walk onto the stage, I see that Ruff's sartorial instinct was correct. Just by their walk—Ruff lugging his bass, Mitchell carrying Ruff's horn—they convey a natural warmth. But what the audience also understands is that they are serious about what they do. The nature of the transaction is established before it starts.

All of Mitchell and Ruff's concerts have the same format, but no two are alike. They never plan their program in advance. After each number Ruff announces what they will play next—a decision that is mainly emotional, growing out of how they feel at the moment. I've heard them play concerts on three successive nights with no duplication. But the framework is constant. Ruff takes care of the amenities and keeps his comments brief, identifying the next song and its composer. At some point he also makes a local reference that acknowledges the town or college that is their host. Mitchell says nothing and never looks at the audience; he is locked into his music.

Ruff always plays his bass for the first two or three numbers, setting a jazz rhythm that compensates for the absence of a drum. Then he changes to the French horn and selects a song with a haunting melodic line—Harold Arlen's "Ill Wind," for instance, or Billy Strayhorn's "Lush Life"—that the French horn almost seems to have been invented for. One secret of the Duo's durability is that it has three instruments, and when the bass begins to wear out its welcome Ruff switches to an instrument that isn't associated with jazz and that has a strong emotional content. Many critics, in fact, call Mitchell-Ruff a "chamber jazz" duo. Ruff also varies the pace by giving Mitchell periodic solos, and as he stands by the piano and listens, though he has been listening to Mitchell since 1946, his face takes on the mixture of pleasure and disbelief that goes with being a Mitchell fan.

Now, on Sunday afternoon in Rock Island, all these processes are at work. The Duo begins with an easygoing number that I don't recognize—"that was a blues that we just made up," Ruff tells the audience—and they're off on a program that is typically fresh in its variety. Mitchell does a complex piano solo of Jerome Kern's "Yesterday"; Ruff joins him with his French horn to play a medley from *Porgy and Bess,* and then the lyrical mood is broken with a romp through Dizzy Gillespie's "Con Alma," Ruff again playing the bass. After that Ruff pauses for a local reference. He remembers that Davenport is the birthplace of Bix Beiderbecke, the great jazz cornetist, and he announces that the next number will be an improvisation called "New Blues for Bix." But first he is diverted by the ghost of Beiderbecke into a brief reminiscence.

"I don't know if young people in this area are as intimidated as I was by growing up in the shadow of a famous person," he says. He explains that Helen Keller came from Tuscumbia, next door to Sheffield, where he grew up, and that she was always being cited by schoolteachers who were impatient with lackadaisical students. "Those teachers would say, 'Aren't you ashamed to be so lazy about your reading? Look at that Keller girl.' Helen Keller made book learning even more distasteful than it was." The story is, to say the least, unexpected. But there is no time to ponder Helen Keller's demoralizing effect on early education; "New Blues for Bix" is under way, and Mitchell begins to roll. He has told Ruff—as he often does—that he doesn't want to break the momentum with an intermission, and he builds to a brilliant treatment of "Autumn Leaves" in three-quarter time. When it's over, Ruff says, "I have seldom heard this young man so energetic so early in the day. There must be something in that Mississippi River water he's been drinking over at the Blackhawk Hotel." They wrap it up with "My Old Flame" and the audience is on its feet, clapping and shouting and not wanting it to end.

Afterward, many people come backstage to ask where the Duo will be playing next: instant converts. Mitchell, of course, has no idea—he still hasn't returned from wherever he was during the concert. In fact, after a concert he can never remember what he played. But Ruff knows. "Tuesday night at the John Deere auditorium," he says. A TV reporter asks if he can tape an interview for the evening news. Ruff is tired, but from the thoughtful quality of his answers the man from WHBF wouldn't know it.

We go back to Davenport for a buffet dinner in the home of a doctor who is on the board of Visiting Artists. The dinner is for patrons and potential backers and other influential citizens—about a hundred altogether. Most of them were at the concert and they beard Mitchell and Ruff with obscure questions about jazz that the two men dutifully try to answer.

Soon enough they will be asked to perform. Someone will ask them to play "Star Dust." Probably even Horowitz gets asked to play "Star Dust."

After supper Mitchell and Ruff are pushed to the piano. Playing conditions are hardly ideal: the clink of coffee cups, the hum of conversation from other rooms. But they go to work once more—in the desert of the arts, community involvement is a flower that must be ceaselessly watered. They play several numbers and then a woman catches Mitchell's eye. "Would you play 'Star Dust'?" she says.

Monday

Grant Elementary School, Davenport, 10 A.M. Three hundred children—kindergarten through sixth grade—troop into the gymnasium with their teachers and sit on the floor. Ruff greets them amiably. "First we're going to show you how these instruments sound before we put them together," he says. He holds up his French horn. "The horn wasn't so much invented as it just grew—it grew on animals." He plays a few hunting calls and bugle calls. What the sound conveys is something very old: the horn as one of man's earliest senders of messages. Mitchell plays a major scale and a chromatic scale on the upright piano and explains about the half tones. Ruff asks the kids if they can say "improvisation." They can. "To improvise," he says, "means to have fun with something—to change it around and make it different. You all know the major scale that Mr. Mitchell just played.

Now we're going to play a piece that we call 'Do-Re-Mi Blues' so you can hear what improvisation is."

Mitchell puts the major scale through various lively incarnations, with Ruff on the bass. The children are delighted by how many forms it can take. "That's called jazz," Ruff says. "You should know that nobody else in the world invented jazz but Americans. It's truly American music. It sprang from the soil of your great country and it's one of the riches you should be proud of. If you ever travel outside this country you'll find that people in other lands know this part of your culture because they enjoy it so much."

Ruff asks how many children are studying the piano. Many hands go up. "I am *impressed!*" he says. "Is there somebody here who would like to play a melody for us?" A chubby boy named Jerry Boovey comes to the piano. Ruff asks him what he wants to play. Jerry says he's going to play "Cool School." The piece, a pulsing melody with a boogie bass, is presumably Jerry's conception of school, if not necessarily his teacher's. When it's over, Mitchell leads the applause. Ruff says, "Now Mr. Mitchell is going to take Jerry's piece, 'Cool School,' and make some jazz out of it." Mitchell separates the song into two parts and plays the boogie bass for Ruff. "He just made an arrangement," Ruff explains. "He wants me to play on my bass what Jerry played with his left hand." The song is duly played and embroidered. The children are caught up in it, clapping in rhythm and laughing at the variations. Ruff then talks about "a wonderful American opera that I hope you'll all hear someday, called *Porgy and*

Bess, by a great American composer named George Gershwin." They play some numbers from the wonderful American opera and conclude with a song of Ruff's called "Chou-Chou," which, he explains, is a French term of endearment for pets, little children and old dogs. Mitchell gets a tremendous rhythm going, playing as hard as I've ever heard him play.

Ruff asks if anyone has any questions. One girl says she plays the cello now but would also like to play the bass. Ruff assures her that she should be able to learn it quite easily. Someone asks Ruff how he learned to play. He says that at their age he was a drummer, but when he went into the army Mitchell taught him to play the bass. "If I played any wrong notes he'd hit me and make me stand in the corner on one leg," Ruff says, "so I made sure I learned fast." A boy raises his hand: "How come the French horn sounds like a moose?" Ruff speculates briefly on this musical phenomenon. "Time for one more question," he says. A small girl has a question, and Ruff leans forward to hear it. "When he hit you," she says, pointing to Mitchell, "did you bleed?"

The hour is up and the teachers herd the children out. Two undergraduates from Blackhawk Junior College's educational television center have been taping the class and they conclude it by interviewing Mitchell and Ruff. The program will be shown on cable TV and will also be available as a research tool in local colleges, schools and libraries. Knowing this, the interviewers ask questions that deal with the educational foundations of jazz. Mitchell and Ruff both emphasize their formal training. Mitchell says it's very important to him that his jazz is grounded in classical disciplines. "Can you teach someone to improvise?" the interviewer wants to know. "What I can teach is form and structure," Mitchell says. "When you teach improvisation, your students somehow wind up sounding like you—and that's not good."

The principal of Grant School, Morris Williams, is elated by the visit. "I'm glad to see men musicians come to the school," he says. "At this age boys have a tendency to feel that if they're not athletic there's something wrong with them. I was very athletic when I was a boy. But my son wasn't athletic at all—he was musical and he wanted to play the piano. This bothered me a great deal and there was a lot of conflict between us for a long time—until finally I understood. I understood the great enjoyment and value that he got from music."

• • •

We hurry back to the Blackhawk Hotel for the Monday lunch of the Davenport Rotary Club. It's held in the Gold Room, a vestigial ballroom of the kind that every downtown hotel uses for banquets and conventions. We are at the head table, up on a dais, along with various Rotary officers and committee chairmen. Two hundred Rotarians are seated at round tables. They make an ocean of gray: gray suits and gray faces. We are at the absolute center of the American male experience; no bright shirts or gaudy ties violate its centrality. We stand and sing "America." We bow our heads for a prayer that gives thanks for the opportunity to do good work. We eat a plain meal that is served with a minimum of fuss. Announcements are made. Guests are introduced: Mitchell, Ruff, sons home from college, members from other chapters. Applause is polite. A few jokes are made by the chairman. Laughter is dutiful.

Mitchell and Ruff have been given only twenty minutes to perform: they are booked for a TV program in the early afternoon. They crank themselves up and play. But there are no signs of life in the Gold Room. Nothing comes back from the 200 men at the tables; their emotions are as neatly buttoned as their suits. But the concert ends and they stand up and cheer. They look happy and somehow they also look younger. Lunch is adjourned, but the men don't leave. They make their way to the dais to thank Mitchell and Ruff for coming. "It makes a big difference in the week," one of them says.

We leave the Blackhawk and drive over to Moline, where Mitchell and Ruff rehearse and tape a television show called *Visiting Artists*—some playing and some talk with the host— for WQAD, an ABC station. Because Ruff's bass is so big, every trip requires double transportation. Lois Jecklin drives Mitchell and me in her car, and one of her friends drives Ruff and his bass in a station wagon. At least Ruff always knows what his instruments will sound like. Mitchell never does; every piano is different, and the difference often comes in the form of some terrible surprise. Luckily, the studio piano at WQAD is a good one, and the show goes quite easily. But as Mitchell plays some warm-up scales he is reminded that the piano at yesterday's concert at Augustana College had one note so badly out of tune—the G below middle C—that he couldn't stand it. "I didn't play that note during the whole concert," he tells me. "I had to voice all my chords differently so as not to touch it."

• • •

Lois Jecklin's father was a superintendent of schools in Iowa, and she grew up in many different parts of the state. Her mother was an amateur painter. "When I was in second grade," she recalls, "we lived in a very small town called Missouri Valley. To get art you had to go to Omaha. One Saturday my parents took me to the Joslyn Art Museum in Omaha to see a loan exhibition from the Metropolitan Museum of Art. The Joslyn was a beautiful light-brown marble building, with a pool in the lobby that was full of green plants. We went into a huge oval room that had walls covered in brown silk. Suddenly there was a gigantic painting in front of me— it was Rosa Bonheur's *Horse Fair*—and at that moment I understood the difference between art and what my mother did. It was also my first sense of architecture as a place."

That story multiplied many times is the story of the arts in America. Every community has a Lois Jecklin who is operating out of some early encounter with art or music, or theater or dance, or poetry or fiction, and is trying to weave it into the fabric of her city's life. If the effort fails more often than it succeeds, it's because the business of America is still business, as Calvin Coolidge so bluntly reminded us, and art is something that "artists" do. Still, the Visiting Artist Series is an example of the gains that can be made with perseverance. It grew out of a modest project that the Quad-City Arts Council started in the late 1960s to exhibit the work of local artists, to hold classes and to exchange information through newsletters. In the fall of 1973, Deere & Company was asked if it would sponsor a program to bring performing artists to the community for periods of several months. Deere made a challenge grant, Lois Jecklin became project director, and the residencies were launched. The performers were supplied by Affiliated Artists, an organization long in the business of sending performers to communities across America.

In 1976 the program evolved into a separate creature called Visiting Artist Series, Inc. "We began to obtain performers from other sources and we also changed our format," Mrs. Jecklin says. "Instead of bringing one person to the Quad Cities for eight weeks we started bringing four artists here for two weeks—or, if they were very busy, for one week. We also arrived at a rough formula for dividing the artists' time among the many audiences we wanted them to reach." Today the visiting artists spend fifty percent of their time in schools within a twenty-mile radius, from Clinton to Muscatine; twenty percent in factories and with "forgotten audiences" (men and women in such institutions as halfway houses, prisons and old people's homes); and the rest doing TV programs that the community will see, holding clinics and workshops at the area's seven colleges, and giving free public performances.

Ninety percent of the money is privately raised from local businesses, foundations and individual citizens. (A small amount comes from arts councils and other such funding agencies.) "The people are beginning to be proud of the program," Mrs. Jecklin says. One of her main objectives has been to break down the wall that separates Americans from their art. "Over and over," she says, "artists and writers and composers and musicians come here and tell about themselves and their lives." In many cases the artists also work with their audience. A striking example was the visit of the sculptor Beverly Pepper, who spent her residency in the Deere foundry making two giant sculptures that stayed behind when she left. One, *Trapezium,* is outside the Davenport Art Gallery; the other, *Spirit of Place,* is outside the Deere factory. Miss Pepper collaborated with many men in the foundry: with engineers, with computer technicians who converted her blueprints into specifications for casting, and with the laborers who actually built the two pieces.

"That's the kind of thing that makes enthusiasts out of nonbelievers," Mrs. Jecklin says. "The men in the foundry saw that their skills were needed by a sculptor of world importance to create her art. They could see a direct connection between art and life. Programs like this have given us credibility. People have had art brought to them that they previously avoided because they thought there was nothing in it for them. Now they see that artists are men and women who relate to them in a number of ways, and they've been stretched. They're much more adventurous and curious and open."

She quotes the sculptor Henry Moore, who, she reminds me, was the son of a coal miner: "The city is the house of its inhabitants and should be furnished with works of art."

Tuesday

Three appearances are scheduled for today: in Bettendorf, Rock Island and Moline. Mitchell and Ruff are the first jazz musicians brought here by the Visiting Artist Series, and they are being thinly spread across the Quad Cities.

In midmorning we go to Scott Community College, one of the three branches of Eastern Iowa Community College. Technically it's in Bettendorf, but it's well out in the country-side. The day is cold and the landscape is flat and frozen. Scott is a fairly new campus that looks like every other fairly new campus in America: three or four low redbrick buildings. Mitchell and Ruff are supposed to play at a brown-bag lunch in the student center; the audience can listen while it eats.

The student center is in the basement—a long and ster-ile room with a low ceiling and tile walls. It's very obviously the student center: it has a jukebox, a Ping-Pong table, some video games and several snack and soft-drink machines, all in use. The noise level is high. The average age of the stu-dents is about twenty-eight. Those who aren't playing games or getting food are sitting at metal tables, eating or chatting or studying. Several have their young children with them.

An upright piano is against the far wall, next to the Ping-Pong table, and Mitchell wonders if the Ping-Pong game will stop when he plays. He thinks it probably won't. He tries out the piano and Ruff sets up his bass. They know that it's one of those rooms that will never be entirely still, but they don't seem upset: this is where they are booked to play, and they go to work. It's the week of Duke Ellington's birthday, Ruff tells the students, and he launches into "Satin Doll." The students at the near tables stop eating and listen. Ruff stays with Ellington and plays "Caravan." Mitchell gets into a galloping rhythm and the room becomes quieter. Picking up momentum, the two men play "The More I See You." Mitchell is working hard at the beat-up piano; except in the high notes it sounds almost like a Steinway. He is also playing with great skill—a triumph of art over environment. I'm reminded of the only time I've ever seen Mitchell angry. He said he told one of his students that he had been asked to play at a wedding reception, and the student said the occasion was unworthy of Mitchell's talents. "I told him, 'Don't you even think of ever saying that to me again,'" Mitchell recalled. "It's a privilege to play for people."

Mitchell and Ruff play intently for forty-five minutes. They are sweating with effort; the room is hot, the acoustics are bad, and there's a lot of coming and going. But the students also know that something of quality is taking place. One woman at a nearby table is wholly absorbed in the music. Later she comes up to Mitchell. She is a pianist herself, she says, desperate for contact with the kind of art she has just heard. "You've made my whole year," she tells him.

. . .

We drive back to Davenport for lunch and then go over to Rock Island, where Mitchell and Ruff are scheduled to hold a master class at Augustana College. About thirty undergraduates turn up. Ordinarily these clinics attract student pianists and instrumentalists who want individual criticism. But today we are in for group therapy: a seven-man college combo is setting up its equipment, much of it electronic, including the piano. They call themselves the Six O'Clock Jazz Ensemble and they want to know how they sound. They play two long numbers with grim determination, reading their music as if they were decoding the Dead Sea Scrolls. Mitchell and Ruff look almost as glum.

When the music stops, Ruff steps into the uneasy silence. He asks the drummer to try a samba beat and a higher register to give the group more color and contrast. He urges the non-electrified horn players to think about dynamics and shading. "I'd like you to be more aggressive," he tells the boy with the tenor sax. The boy looks dubious. "Let me hear it again," Ruff says, and the combo plods back into action. The drummer sounds better, but otherwise it's the same old Six O'Clock Jazz Ensemble. After a while Ruff stops them. "I feel that you're holding back," he says. "If you'd dare to be loud and aggressive you'd probably scare yourselves to death." Their faces say that this is unlikely. "Did you ever get in a car and close all the doors and just holler?" Ruff asks. They shake their heads. "It does a world of good in your blues playing."

Ruff and Mitchell play a few numbers for the students and then ask for questions. The students want to know how the two men practice. Ruff says he makes up his own exercises—"a grueling kind of lip calisthenics"—and also plays chamber music. He describes how he has been helped by a teacher in New York named Carmine Caruso, who makes a specialty of "fixing the problems of brass players." Mitchell says that he favors Chopin études as an exercise, and he plays a few passages to demonstrate the kind of intricacy that he means. "You can't do anything without technique—that's what opens you up," he tells the boy who was playing the electric keyboard. "I feel that you're too safe." The boy radiates safety. Finally Mitchell says, "Listen, man, the piano just sits there looking at you all day. You've got to put something in it if you want to get something out."

• • •

Mitchell and Ruff return to the Blackhawk to rest. Then it's time to leave for the Deere headquarters, where tonight's concert will be held. We've heard that the building is one of Eero Saarinen's masterpieces, and we're eager to see it.

John Deere was a Vermont blacksmith who went west in 1836 and settled in the village of Grand Detour, Illinois. He repaired the equipment of the farmers and listened to their complaints, one of which was that the rich Midwestern soil stuck to the bottom of their cast-iron plows and had to be constantly scraped off. Deere designed and began to manufacture a polished steel plow that cut a clean furrow and left the dirt in the ground. Soon he moved his plant to Moline to take advantage of the Mississippi River for power and transportation. He began to import rolled steel from England and by 1843 he was making a thousand plows a year.

In 1955 a newly installed Deere president, William Hewitt, felt that a new headquarters was needed. His vision for the company was one of growth and excellence, and downtown Moline was too cramped for the kind of building he had in mind. He decided to build out in the Illinois countryside— a move that he knew the people of Moline might resent— and he began studying the work of various architects. One of the buildings he visited was Saarinen's General Motors Technical Center, near Detroit, which had just been completed. Saarinen, he decided, was the man he wanted.

He invited the architect to Moline and the two men went out to see four tracts of land that Deere had scouted. All of them were hilly and quite heavily wooded, and Hewitt borrowed a utility company's "cherry picker" that had a thirty-five-foot tower. From that perch the president and the architect looked out over the contours of the land, and Saarinen chose a seven-hundred-acre parcel. Deere acquired the property over the next year and Saarinen came back to decide where to place the building. What Hewitt wanted was an administration center for a thousand people that would also have a four-hundred-seat auditorium and an exhibition hall for displaying Deere's farm machines, all under one roof. Saarinen chose a site that straddled a small ravine and had a view across the Rock River valley. For his main material he chose a steel called Cor-Ten that would rust and have a rugged outdoor look appropriate to a company that works the land.

Saarinen's design was approved by the board in 1961; three weeks later he died suddenly at the age of fifty-two. The building opened in 1964 and was an immediate hit, not only with architecture critics, who honored it with various awards, but with the local farmers. Far from regarding it as a showy extravagance and a desertion of the city, they took pride in the building and brought their families from great distances to see it. Today the building and its art collection attract almost 100,000 visitors a year.

"William Hewitt had a sense of the possible," Lois Jecklin says as she drives us out from Moline, "and he was willing to gamble. Moving out here was a symbolic act—he wanted the building to say, 'We are an important company whose interest is in quality.' He was a man who liked to create an opening so that other people could have their vision. One way he did it was to encourage the arts. Another way was to create this building. It has raised the consciousness of the whole area."

The Deere building is about ten miles outside of town. It's a wide box, seven stories high, and from the highway it looks to us like many other corporate glass offices. But it doesn't dwarf its setting; it sits in harmonious balance with its landscape and its two man-made lakes. When we get out of the car and walk toward the building it loses its glassiness and becomes a work of steel—linear and strong. Inside, Ruff feels right at home. We have stepped into a giant exhibition space that's full of Deere farm machines, all of them different, going back to one of the founder's first plows. Ruff's thoughts are on the land that he used to work as a boy in Alabama, where he says everybody used Deere tractors.

The building delights us with its light and space. It's one of those buildings in which every detail is right. Above all, it's right as a place for people to work in. The halls are wide, and at every turn there seems to be a window. Many of the window offices are for employees who do typing and filing; the beautiful view is a shared right, not an executive privilege.

So is the art. Saarinen intended the walls to be blank: he wanted the building and its occupants to constitute the art. Hewitt disagreed, and in his travels to overseas branches of Deere he assembled a collection that is surprising in its richness and variety. The most famous of its six hundred pieces is homegrown—Grant Wood's *Fall Plowing*—and so are the stunning Edward Curtis photographs of American Indians that line one long corridor. But otherwise the works are resolutely international. Chagall prints, Brazilian paintings, Peruvian tapestries, Japanese screens, Thai temple doors, Oceanic tribal masks, Roman glass, medieval English embroidery— every wall is both a pleasure and an education. I'm struck, as I have been in other corners of America, by the difference that one man and one company can make in the quality of life.

. . .

Mitchell and Ruff go to the auditorium early to look it

over. It's handsome, like the rest of the building, but with the intimacy of a small concert hall. Backstage, it has a door big enough for the biggest combine to drive through—this theater can present a full cast of Deere's green and yellow tractors, works of art in themselves.

The piano is an almost new seven-foot grand, and Mitchell tries it out before he even takes off his coat. It hasn't been tuned. "The piano's got eight A's, all different," he tells me. Ruff is hailed from the highest tier by a young man who says he will be operating the lights. Ruff shouts up to him that whatever he wants to do will be fine. The hall begins to fill up with men and women who have driven out from the Quad Cities. I recognize quite a few who were at the Sunday afternoon concert. Lois Jecklin works the house, asking the new arrivals whether they are on the mailing list of Visiting Artists. They gladly fill out a card for her; in America the arts have one sacred text—the mailing list.

The concert seems sluggish at first. After one or two numbers I hear where the trouble is: the piano is dead. It's a factory lemon from a famous factory. Mitchell is probing the keyboard like a doctor examining a dying patient for some sign of life. He plays at different registers and different volumes, searching for any group of notes where the piano may have some strength or will at least sound decent. Eventually he finds it in the octave below middle C. Playing quite softly, in a style that emphasizes chords rather than rhythm, he coaxes a chamber music effect out of the piano. Ruff, perhaps by intuition, has switched instruments early and is having a fabulous night on the French horn. He plays three plaintive songs—Harold Arlen's "Last Night When We Were Young," Billy Strayhorn's "Lush Life" and Jerome Moross's "Lazy Afternoon"—with an intensity of emotion that I have rarely heard him bring to a concert. The audience becomes caught up in what he is doing, and even Mitchell claps with admiration.

Meanwhile, the young man on the lights has gone color-crazy. Cued by the mood of each song, he bathes Mitchell and Ruff in blues and reds and purples—every color except the one that gives elegance to an evening of music, especially one that involves black musicians and black and white evening clothes and a black instrument with black and white keys. The eye yearns for ordinary light, and so, I realize, does the ear; color is a powerful mood changer, and it seems to muffle the sound, doubling Mitchell's handicap at the muffled piano. The result is a concert totally different from the one on Sunday afternoon. It has a lyrical quality, and the audience, oblivious of the burden that the two men have overcome and turned to their advantage, is having a wonderful time. The applause is long and loud.

At several points Ruff talks to the audience. He praises Lois Jecklin and the Quad Cities for their Visiting Artist Series. At another point he acknowledges his corporate host —stopping, however, well short of solemnity. "Seeing this beautiful building from the highway," he says, "inspired us to write a song. It took me back to my Alabama boyhood when I used to plow with a mule, and this is the piece that we composed as we walked through the door." He starts plucking his bass and he and Mitchell ramble through an amiable blues. By the end of the night Mitchell has bent the piano to his will and he builds "I'll Remember April" to a climax that brings the audience to its feet. As the two men take a bow the stage is suddenly lit in white. Ruff looks up to the top tier as if to say "*Now* you get it right!" But what he says is "Let's have a hand for the young man up there who did such a fine job on the lights." The audience is as high as the young man on the lights. Mitchell and Ruff are not. It's been a long, hard day in the Quad Cities.

Wednesday

America is dotted with palatial homes that were built by industrial barons in the golden age of free enterprise and that have since been converted into schools or colleges. This morning we are in one of them—a twenty-eight-room mansion, on a bluff overlooking the Mississippi River at Bettendorf, that is now occupied by St. Katharine's/St. Mark's School. It was built by Joseph Bettendorf, one of two brothers who gave the town its name and its main employment. Originally Joseph and William Bettendorf owned a wagon factory in Davenport. In the early 1900s it burned down and they went to the neighboring village of Gilbert with a proposition. If the citizens would buy the old Gilbert farm along the river, the Bettendorfs would build a new factory there. The people duly raised the money, and their reward was that the Bettendorf Company grew into one of America's biggest manufacturers of railroad cars. Its success was based on William Bettendorf's invention of a one-piece truck—the frame under each end of a railroad car that holds the wheels in place. It became the prototype for the trucks that were used on all American freight cars, and, needless to say, the Bettendorf brothers prospered. The village of Gilbert became the town of Bettendorf, and both men built homes worthy of their new wealth.

Now Ruff is unpacking his bass in what was once the library—one of four elegant downstairs rooms, the others being a living room, a formal dining room and a conservatory with a stained-glass dome. (The ninety-foot ballroom on the third floor is still intact, but the two bowling alleys in the basement have been turned into a science lab.) Nothing was skimped on the interiors: we are surrounded by Italian marble fireplaces, carved woodwork, ornate paneling and molded plaster. But the school has not been intimidated by the house; it has settled into the rooms and given them an informality that they probably didn't have when the Bettendorfs were entertaining railroad executives from the East.

St. Katharine's/St. Mark's is a private school that runs from the preschool years up to college. It was founded one hundred years ago in Davenport as a boarding and day school for Christian young women, and today it is the only survivor of the many seminaries and academies in Iowa that provided a formal secondary education before the era of public schools. In 1968 it went coeducational and added St. Mark's to its name; in 1973 it moved into the Bettendorf mansion, and its present enrollment is two hundred and fifty. For this morning's Mitchell-Ruff visit the student body has been divided into younger and older groups, and now the children from kindergarten through sixth grade arrive and sit on the floor.

Mitchell and Ruff perform and explain jazz for almost an hour. When Ruff asks for a volunteer to play a melody that they can improvise on, a boy comes to the piano and plays "Old MacDonald Had a Farm." Mitchell's first chorus comes out sounding like Palestrina—maybe it's all that Italian marble—and then he and Ruff take the old nursery song through a meandering journey. Finally the younger grades are shepherded out, the kids from grades seven through twelve troop in, and a new session begins. When the time comes for questions, the students don't want to know about the music as much as they want to know about the musicians. Who are these two genial strangers who have dropped into their midst? They ask how old Mitchell and Ruff are, and where they grew up, and how they learned to play their instruments, and where they live now, and where they teach, and what countries they have toured. One girl asks Ruff how many languages he can speak. "As many as I want to eat in," he replies. But the girl wants a better answer. Ruff says that he can speak French, Italian, Spanish, Portuguese, German, Russian and Chinese and that this has helped him to tell audiences all over the world about American jazz. But he and Mitchell are glad to be in the Quad Cities, he says, and for their final number they're going to play a special composition.

It's called "The Bettendorf Stomp, Breakdown and Git Back."

• • •

Nowhere are the two men more different than in what they do when a performance is over. By metabolism, Mitchell is a purebred artist, acutely tuned to his senses and his body. He lives close to the elemental forces: food, fatigue, sleep, germs, weather, people, the discomforts of travel. He forgets names, places, dates, papers, possessions and other mundane details. "The spirits will take care of it," he says. "If it's meant to happen it will."

Ruff has no such faith in predestination. If it happens it's because he *makes* it happen. Ruff puts every minute to work. On airplanes and in airports he is always reading a book. In his hotel room he is the ant laying up provisions for the season ahead; there is nothing of the grasshopper in him. Before breakfast this morning he was up practicing Mozart's Second Concerto for Orchestra and French Horn, which he will play with the Boston Classical Orchestra in May. He was accompanied by an add-a-part tape of the concerto, which, like his tape recorder, he had remembered to bring along. (Mitchell left his glasses in Alabama on Sunday and mislaid his wallet yesterday.)

Now, in his room at the Blackhawk, Ruff turns into a booking agent. He has his engagement calendar open for both 1983 and 1984 and he starts to return the phone calls that came for him while he was at the school in Bettendorf. Bill Cosby is doing a two-week stand at Las Vegas and wants the Mitchell-Ruff Duo to open his act. Ruff likes the idea for practical reasons: the pay and the exposure are good. Mitchell, lying on the bed, dislikes the idea for emotional reasons. Opening Cosby's act would mean doing two twenty-minute stints—one early in the evening and one late—and he would have to be "up" from the very first chord. He prefers a longer time to build his transaction with the audience. Besides, who needs Las Vegas?

I think of all the rooms where Mitchell and Ruff have stayed since they were discovered by the Pryor-Menz Agency in 1955. Even then the agency was an old one—it had been in business since the nineteenth century, when it booked authors like Mark Twain on lecture tours. Now it wanted two personable young musicians who could play and explain jazz on college campuses. The two young musicians will never forget the first day they went out on the circuit.

"The Pryor-Menz office was in Council Bluffs, Iowa," Mitchell says, "and we left from there by train with the tickets and the itinerary that the agency had given us. We were going to play at Hays College in Hays, Kansas. The train conductor was a black man, and he looked and looked at our tickets. 'You sure you boys are going to *Hays?*' he said. We said we were. He said he had been on that railroad line for thirty-three years and no black people had ever got off at Hays. We told him we were supposed to play at Hays College. 'Well, I'm going to hold the train,' he said, 'until I'm sure you're in the right place. If there's nobody there to meet you at the depot you're going to get back on the train.' Well, we got off at Hays and looked around, and that conductor stood right there on the steps of the train watching us. Finally we saw this white man come driving up in a station wagon. It was the president of Hays College and he had come to meet us. The conductor couldn't believe his eyes, and he kept the train right there until we got in that station wagon and drove off. As the train pulled out he was still standing there on the steps looking back."

The solicitude of black trainmen for black people traveling on the trains was a gift that Ruff still talks about warmly. But the biggest problem for black entertainers before the civil rights movement was where to spend the night. "Pryor-Menz always sent us out with this huge book full of names of people who would give room and board to black musicians," Ruff recalls, "and with lists of hotels where it was O.K. to eat in the dining room, or where you had to have your meals sent up, or where you couldn't get served at all. The people who put you up in their homes were black doctors and dentists and preachers, and for many of them it was a good steady income. We would set out from Pryor-Menz with this book of names and with a fistful of train tickets and a Conoco credit card. If we were going to a town where the trains didn't go, they'd give us a V-8 Ford. When we got back to a place that had a railroad, somebody would collect the Ford and presumably drive it back to Council Bluffs. It was all worked out with the most meticulous instructions."

Meanwhile, an agency in Atlanta that was almost equally old, called Alkahest, signed Mitchell and Ruff to tour the

Southern states east of the Mississippi, which were not Pryor-Menz territory, and it still books them today. (Pryor-Menz has since folded.) Originally, *Alkahest* was a literary magazine, but it soon ran out of money to pay its authors, so it sent them off to lecture for a fee instead. Such was the appeal of live talent that by 1920 the head of Alkahest, S. Russell Bridges, had 165 chautauqua towns in Georgia alone where he booked speakers, magicians, singers, pianists, male quartets and other such entertainers. Today the descendants of those audiences are at home watching television, and the challenge is to find acts that will lure them out. The present head of Alkahest, Ralph Bridges, who is Russell's son, told me that Mitchell and Ruff always draw an eager crowd but that sure winners nowadays are rare. This came up indirectly when I asked him where the agency got its name. "You'll find the word 'alkahest' in most dictionaries," he said. "It's the universal solvent—the pot of gold at the end of the rainbow that the ancient alchemists were looking for. I can assure you that it has nothing to do with our present financial situation."

Mitchell and Ruff like to play at colleges because it's a way of bringing jazz to a generation that they feel is deprived. "American students," Ruff says, "don't know the same things that students in Shanghai don't know—where jazz comes from and what it is. Whenever we visit a college we have a limited amount of time, so we want to leave as much information as we can." Traditionally, young people learned about jazz by listening to the great artists in New York clubs. "Big-name stars like Miles Davis, Louis Armstrong and Erroll

Garner would play New York at least once a year," Ruff points out, "to keep their name before an audience that was important. But today there's such a saturation of electronic music that the public is gone and great musicians don't think club exposure does them any good. You don't see a 'first team' anymore in New York clubs—there's no Ella, no Miles, no Oscar Peterson, no Sarah Vaughan. And that's devastating to musically gifted youngsters because that's where the great jazz artists really learned what they know. As a jazz center where big names play, New York is Peoria finally."

. . .

After lunch Mitchell and Ruff head out once more. Lois Jecklin notices the onset of fatigue and apologizes for booking them so heavily; next time she'll know better. The afternoon workshop is at Seton Catholic School in Moline: 125 students of grades six through eight.

Then it's back to the hotel to get ready for tonight's public concert in Eldridge, Iowa, twenty miles away. The day has turned cold; snow is falling, and a wind off the river is blowing white gusts through the empty streets of Davenport. Cars are starting to skid and the radio is telling people to stay home unless they absolutely have to go out.

Mitchell and Ruff change into their tuxedos and a young woman from Eldridge arrives in her van to get them. The van is big enough to hold all of us and Ruff's bass, and we start out into the night, nervous about the icy roads. But our driver knows all about Iowa winters; she is calm and competent. Rural Iowa, however, is nowhere in sight—the road leading out of the Quad Cities is the same road that leads out of Tampa and Tulsa and Topeka and all the other cities in America, a strip of taco huts and pizza huts and shopping malls. At last the clutter thins out and a sign announces that we are entering Eldridge. As we cross the railroad tracks at the edge of town I see a huge grain elevator. We are in the heartland! America is not one big taco hut after all.

A small theater designed with considerable flair has just opened as an annex of North Scott High School, in the middle of Eldridge, and there the community hopes to plant the flag of the performing arts. It's called the Countryside Theater, and its president, Phyllis Green, an elementary school writing teacher, is at the front door watching the families that are materializing out of the night and shaking off the snow. Mrs. Green says that she and her fellow volunteers don't think the arts should take root only in cities, like Davenport, that are some distance away. They should be available to people who live in rural areas. Her committee is trying to rally enough support in the county to bring good artists to the Countryside Theater throughout the year. The Joffrey Ballet, in fact, will be coming next month. "We don't know if we can get enough people interested," she says. "All I know is that the only way to find out is to try."

Tonight's turnout is encouraging: the theater is more than half full despite the bad weather, and the audience has an enthusiasm that transmits itself to Mitchell and Ruff. They respond with unusual warmth, generating a sunny mood and playing for almost two hours. Even in Eldridge, Ruff is not stuck for a local reference. "Because your town shares its name with a distinguished jazz trumpeter," he says, "this is a blues that we dedicate to you—and to Roy."

Among the people who come backstage afterward is an early fan of the Mitchell-Ruff Duo, and he has brought a record album that the Duo made in 1956, to be autographed. On the front of the jacket is a photograph of two happy-go-lucky kids. The bass player looks about sixteen and is smiling from ear to ear. The pianist is a tall, thin and handsome young man, and both of them are on top of the world.

Thursday

The final day begins at Pleasant Valley High School, in nearby Pleasant Valley, Iowa, where Mitchell and Ruff play for 800 students of grades nine through twelve. At the end they are given a "Certificate of Appreciation" by the Quad Cities community in a brief ceremony that surprises and pleases them. But they are visibly running out of energy when they get into the car that takes us to Grant Elementary School in Rock Island.

There is something different about the school that makes its presence felt right away. Rock Island is the most depressed of the Quad Cities, and Grant School—which is almost entirely black—is at the edge of poverty. Budget cuts have eliminated the arts programs that once gave some margin to the school day, and visiting artists are no part of the pupils' lives. Now 500 boys and girls file into the gymnasium and see two visiting artists. They sit on the gym floor and look up expectantly.

Ruff establishes instant contact with them—making them laugh, telling them about the origins of jazz, explaining the structure of the blues, getting them involved in the music they are about to hear. When he and Mitchell start to play, the kids are turned on as if by a switch. It's not only that their faces and bodies come alive; there is an intensity in the way they strain forward to listen to Ruff's bass and to watch Mitchell's hands. Mitchell can feel the energy, though he never looks up. He plays with total commitment. Whatever is happening on the gymnasium floor is connected to the small boy in Dunedin who was Ivory Mitchell, Jr.

The session continues for almost an hour, and at the end Mitchell is drained. "I'm turned on emotionally when I play," he explains, "and kids respond to me because of that, whereas with adults you have to build and take them someplace. I play for children the way I'd play for the biggest grown-up audience anywhere. I change nothing! When I perform I'm transformed into something else. Once you start to touch on yourself you touch other people. But it has to have fire. It has to have meaning. It has to have living—all the things that I've gone through and that I'm sure everyone else has."

• • •

After lunch Mitchell and Ruff crank up their strength

one last time. The final event is a voluntary assembly in Moline High School, and the huge auditorium is jammed to capacity. To amuse so many teen-agers in the early afternoon is no simple task, but Ruff has them quieted down from the start. He's not lecturing to them; he's *talking* to them about music that is important to him and Mitchell, and when they start to play that music—"Satin Doll," "Chou-Chou," "The More I See You," "Con Alma" and several other songs—the students know that they are being told a serious story, and they match it with a seriousness of their own.

When the hour is over I meet the associate principal, Mary Foster. She is a woman whose face is the summing up of what has always been the best of American public education: she would be cast as an associate principal in any movie of the Midwest, such as *Picnic.* Her brown eyes have a warmth and an intelligence that tell me she has spent thousands of hours in classrooms and assemblies and is a shrewd judge of what she sees. "These two men are what it's all about," she says. "It's almost impossible to hold the attention of nine hundred students for an hour in an auditorium as big as this one. But did you notice that there was no talking and no noise and no moving around? Mr. Ruff had a total presence that very few people have when they're up on a stage. He held them with a low volume of sound and with minimal body gestures—which is the antithesis of what today's students are used to. Most entertainers need flashing lights and a volume of sound that's beyond comfort to get students' attention. And when *we* want their attention we yell at them.

"This is an audience that desperately needs to listen. Young people are exposed to a great deal of competing sound and noise and other stimuli; they have precious little experience at listening for 'What is your message to me?' Simple instructions don't get to them. We have to spend a lot of time just preparing them to be receptive. Today I heard selective listening.

"Students at this age are not reliable judges of the middle range of quality. But if something is *good* they recognize it instantly. And it doesn't have to be their kind of music. In fact, what they heard today *isn't* their kind of music—their musical tastes are very diverse. They also recognize what's bad. They're constantly being exposed to entertainers with gimmicks—adults who wear medallions and designer jeans and other symbols that are 'in' with teen-agers and who laboriously go after their approval. There's nothing worse than a pseudo attempt to be one of the kids. There are enough kids.

"Mitchell and Ruff know who they are from the moment they walk on the stage. They're not going to make an effort to ingratiate themselves. Young people are sensitive to that kind of insincerity—they've had a lot of it on TV, and they've had enough. These kids are impressed by anyone who doesn't have to prove himself. I felt that with Mitchell and Ruff we were in the presence of men who have reached for the stars, and I'd guess some of the depths. I'm not surprised that they appealed to the Chinese. Their appeal is universal."

6 . . . New York

Dwike Mitchell lives in an apartment on Central Park West with an aging Steinway grand piano and a new seven-foot Baldwin that he was given in 1982 when he was named a Baldwin Artist. He is a man with many friends—they telephone at all hours, from all over the country, to check in. (Mitchell was married and divorced some years ago.) When he's not on the road with Ruff he spends his days practicing. He gets to the piano around ten A.M. and stays there for as long as six hours. He begins with intensive exercises. Chopin is one of his main workouts. He will start with a Chopin étude in C and play it successively in every key until he gets back to C. "It's just to take you through the keys so that you can get between the cracks and see how everything relates," he says. Even Chopin might quail at the patterns that this exercise imposes on the fingers. But Mitchell has no fear of black keys. In fact, he dislikes the key of C because all the white notes keep his hands too level; he prefers the peaks and valleys of D flat, or E flat, or A flat. Another typical exercise for Mitchell is to take what Chopin wrote for the right hand and play it with his left hand.

Several hours of such masochism leave him feeling toned

up and ready to work on a new song for some future concert. It's not a question of learning the song; he already knows
most of the great ones. The challenge is to give the song a
series of lives that it had never had before, without violating
its identity, and he will labor for days over one that engages
his ear and his mind. Almost any of Harold Arlen's ballads
will do—"Sleepin' Bee," for instance, or "Out of This World";
they come already furnished with a bewitching melody and
a rich harmonic structure. To hear Mitchell dress an Arlen
ballad in a new wardrobe is one of the pleasures of my life,
Arlen being my favorite songwriter and Mitchell my favorite
pianist. Each chorus that Mitchell plays has a different feeling, the difference being in the emotional nature of the
chords. The chords themselves are like nobody else's—elegant, surprising and yet apt; the ear never rejects them as
"wrong." Beyond that, the chords in each chorus are inti-
mately related to each other in how they are voiced. They
form a line and tell a story; they aren't just showy chords
plunked into someone else's song. The composer (whoever
it is) is never harmed.

It was to try to understand how the ear arrives at such
destinations that I began taking lessons from Mitchell in
1980, and I've been going to the apartment on Central Park
West ever since. Mitchell is to me what "Mr. Bill" Anderson
was to him as a young boy in Dunedin. I hear chords coming out of his piano that make me quiver. No matter how
many complex chords I already knew or have since learned,
there is no end of new ones: chords that I never imagined

and would never be able to find by myself. When I learn a new chord on Mitchell's piano I still can't believe that it will also exist on *my* piano, and I hurry home to try it out. But every discovery raises new questions. Having learned a chord that's exactly right for a certain song in a certain key, I'm eager to own it in every other key, and I start by transposing it up a halftone, or down, and it disappears: a shift of only half a tone has robbed it of whatever made it unique. I bring this mystery to Mitchell and he says, "That chord only works in D flat." His ear knows what every chord sounds like in every key at every register. "It's the vibrations," he says. "How the notes vibrate against each other is always different." He talks a lot about vibrations. When he and I analyze chords we are like two lepidopterists poring over a tray of brilliant butterflies, delighting in their infinite variety and their subtle gradations of color. Mitchell also talks a lot about pressure: the pressure of the fingers on the keys. I've begun to hear how a chord can sound wrong in any number of ways, even when the notes are correct, and how Mitchell's chords always sound right. He also talks about posture—the stillness of Horowitz is a marvel to him. Most of all, he talks about feeling. He often mentions some pianist who was technically flawless but who "might as well have not played at all." Emotion, to him, is the crucial ingredient, and music is a total commitment. In his conversation and his concerns I glimpse what it is to be an artist and not just a musician.

There was a time when Mitchell himself was just a

musician. Then he met the person who pushed him beyond that border.

. . .

After Mitchell got out of the army in 1950 he went to Trenton and lived with his aunt. Though he had learned a great deal about music, he still felt that he knew almost nothing about the piano. "It's all very well to learn jazz from jazz musicians," he says, "but ultimately it's impossible for them to teach you anything about *your* instrument. I wanted to begin to deal with the piano from a classical standpoint. I wanted to learn what that instrument was really about. In Trenton a bunch of us used to hang out at the same place having Cokes and beer—we were all very young—and one of the guys, John Santay, was very interested in classical music. One day he insisted that I go to Philadelphia with him to hear the Philadelphia Orchestra. He even bought my railroad ticket. We got to the concert, and this little tiny woman came out on the stage and played a Bach concerto, and I instantly felt this magic bond with what she was doing. I understood her emotions *exactly*. She was playing Bach, but she made me think of Negro spirituals. That did something to me. I found out that her name was Agi Jambor, and that she was Hungarian, and that her husband and her son had both been killed during the war—one was a scientist and the other was a pilot—and that she herself had been imprisoned. She must have been about fifty. I learned that she was teaching at the Philadelphia Musical Academy, and I decided to check it out.

I didn't think I had the ability to attend a conservatory, but I just had the nerve to try. I told the admissions people, 'I'm only going to come here if I can study with Agi Jambor.' And they said, 'She only takes special students.' And I said, 'I'm special—I know nothing.'"

An audition was arranged. Mitchell didn't have anything prepared. He says, "I was getting ready for the biggest kick-out of my life: 'You have my blessing, but please leave.' I played something for this tiny woman and the first thing she said was, 'Where are you from? Tell me about yourself.' She had a very thick accent. I told her I was born in a town in Florida that was so small it had nobody to teach me, but that I had this great feeling for music and I always wanted to know what it was all about. She said, 'You came to the right place.'"

Mitchell moved to Philadelphia and enrolled at the academy, a venerable institution on Rittenhouse Square. He was a full-time student for three and a half years, taking courses in harmony, theory, solfeggio and "everything that everybody else took." His urge to study with Agi Jambor was more than amply gratified. He attended group classes that she taught in such subjects as the musical styles of different composers, and he also took individual piano lessons from her. But that wasn't all. "She'd call me after school three or four times a week and say 'Come on over,'" Mitchell recalls. "That lady was on me all the time. I really think I was her favorite student. I certainly never saw any other students at her house.

"She'd give me skimmed milk and tea biscuits and then

she would play for me. She played mostly Bach, but also quite a bit by Bartók, whom she had known personally. She'd say, 'Listen to this. This is *le-ga-to*—you do not understand it.' And she'd play and I could *hear* it, but I could never quite get it. I used to play so badly when I played classical music for her, and she always said, 'I know you can do it.' She always told me that. She worked so hard with me. She would sit at one piano and I would sit at the other, and we'd play the very same notes, and hers would come out much different and fabulously beautiful. I understand now what I was doing so totally wrong then. A lot of it had to do with how I thought about the instrument in relation to myself. I was going through a good deal of turmoil at the time, and she'd call my father in Florida, and she'd call my mother, and she'd write them letters. I'm blessed to have gotten that kind of attention from someone who was so special. I give her credit for everything I know about how to make sound come out of a piano."

But Mitchell also taught the teacher. "I would play jazz for her, because it was the only thing I could do well," he says, "and she went crazy over it. She said, 'How do you do that? You just think of these things and they come from your head?' I said, 'Well, that's the way we learn.' One Sunday I decided I wanted her to see for herself, so I took her to a Sanctified church in Philadelphia, and she never forgot it. She really cried during the service. She said she had never had an experience that made her feel so strongly about certain things within herself." During those years Mitchell also had a job playing from five to eight in Barney Zeeman's, a restaurant across the street from the Shubert Theater that was a watering hole for theater people who were in town with a pre-Broadway tryout show. But Agi Jambor never came to hear him; she couldn't stand the idea of people talking while someone was playing the piano.

Inevitably, the day came when Mitchell had to play a classical piece in a performance at the academy. "It was Khachaturian's Piano Concerto," he says, "and it was the first piece I had ever played well, because Agi had worked and worked with me. But I was a nervous wreck when it was time to go out on the stage. I was standing there in the wings, and I was so frightened, and I said, 'I'm not going out there.' Agi said, 'You're going—don't worry about it.' Just as I was starting out on the stage, shaking in my boots, she kicked me in the ass just as hard as she could possibly kick. I've never had such a shock. It just blipped out all that nervousness. That was the sendoff she gave me. The next day the critic for the Philadelphia newspaper gave me the write-up of write-ups. I still have it somewhere; it's all yellow and torn."

The after-school sessions are still clear in Mitchell's memory. "Agi's house had a very European feeling," he says. "It had a lot of paintings but hardly anything else; she only had pianos. She was a very attractive woman—very small-faced, with keen features, but she had strength. Her hands were tiny, but they were accurate, and she had all these little things she had devised that enabled her to play pieces that only bigger hands were meant to play, like Bartók's Third Piano Concerto and Chopin's C Major Étude. She invented ways of getting there. She had an active career as a concert pianist and would go off periodically to play with major orchestras like the Chicago Symphony and the New York Philharmonic. Later she married Claude Rains, the actor.

"For three and a half years she played for me a lot—always with explanations. She talked a great deal about certain styles of classical music, and how it's done, and how it's structured, and how it's thought about, and what you must do to make a particular sound on the piano. What I learned from her was totally instrumental—what she knew about that keyboard that I needed to know. The piano is a European instrument that has to be played in a certain way. She didn't influence how I play jazz, which is very individual and which depends on the ear. What I *hear* is one thing, but my touch is directly traceable to her. I want the jazz that I play to be on the highest level that I can attain. I want it to be the epitome of what the piano is all about. Jazz has gone beyond just a little riff; it's really not even 'folk' anymore—it's a true art, and if you're going to do it, get it right. I would hate to go through my life just coming down on those keys and not realizing that if I do *this* I'm going to get *that* as a sound.

"I knew that I had to learn about classical music in order to grow as a jazz pianist. If your ideas are going to expand, then you will have to expand physically. Because if you can't physically do it, forget about your mind."

• • •

Mitchell's next chunk of education was a far cry from skimmed milk and tea biscuits. When he finished school in Philadelphia he went to visit his mother in Jacksonville, and while he was there Lionel Hampton's band came to town. Hampton had heard Mitchell at Lockbourne and told him he wanted him as his pianist when he got out of the army. Instead Mitchell pursued his studies. Now it was almost five years later and he was sure Hampton wouldn't remember him. But he attended Hampton's concert, and afterward, he says, "I went up to him very meekly and said, 'Hello, Lionel.' He took one look at me and said, 'You're the man I want to see. I want you to go with me.' I joined his band two weeks later in Baton Rouge and stayed for two years. We traveled all over Europe and to Israel, and of course that was tremendously broadening for me."

But the main lesson that Mitchell learned from Hampton's band was what it means to be a professional musician. "Unlike the army, where you're fed and taken care of, or the conservatory, which is sheltered, you get the first taste of what it's like to go out and play for thousands and thousands of people who paid to get in," Mitchell says. "You learn about life—about living—very quickly, especially because you do so much traveling. A real closeness develops among the musicians because there are a lot of tight moments financially, and you help each other out.

"I also learned a great deal about show business: matters

of pacing and programming and variety and climaxes. Hampton had a great feeling for that, and it's well worth knowing. He had different things that he did for different audiences in different parts of the world. Wherever he went he would feel out the audience, and by the time he had played two tunes he knew how to put the whole program together. He knew the right thing to do at the right moment.

"Hampton was the rock 'n' roller of jazz—his audiences used to tear the hall apart. In fact, the audiences at rock concerts never acted as wild as the people did when I was in Hampton's band. We played in one of the grandest halls in Vienna—it was a place where Chopin played, you can imagine the grandeur of it—and the audience went out of its mind screaming and tore up the seats. Another time we were playing in Copenhagen and they had let too many people in. The place was literally jumping, and suddenly the floor gave way and all these throngs of people just disappeared. The piano I was playing started to roll right off the stage. I got off that stool fast.

"Hampton was a good vibraphonist and he knew how to take the tempo up and up if he needed to. After so many years you know when you're not making it and you know what to do about it."

• • •

Mitchell doesn't think of himself as a teacher in any formal sense, and he has never gone looking for business. All his students have been people who came to him and asked to be taught. "I've never had a student yet that I taught the same," he says. "I build on what I find. Every one of my students has had something special, but they were special in different ways."

A boy named Andy, for instance, is never far from his thoughts. "Andy came closest to being my child," Mitchell says. "In a way he *is* my child. There were so many things he had to fight—things in his background that kept him from playing—and we fought those things together. When I met him he was about sixteen. He couldn't find where he belonged; he thought his parents hated him—they kept telling him he was a nobody—and he hated *them*. He let his hair grow long and he grew a beard and he looked terrible. When he first came to me I said, 'Listen, you can't come here with all that stuff hanging on you. You've got to cut *something*.' He always had the most rejected look on his face. If you said, 'Andy, don't do it that way; play it this way,' his face would contort and he'd look so hurt and he'd start to cry. Finally I said, 'I'm not telling you this to hurt you—I only want you to play it right, and you have to understand that, and if you have to cry over *that,* then you have to cry.'

"He never had much money, but he'd always bring health foods. He'd go to a commune and buy tons of stuff. He'd bring me brown rice, and I loved it. He never came empty-handed; I have drawers filled with things he's given me. He gave me my piano bench. I had been sitting on a stool that was no bigger than a biscuit, with two pillows on top of it, and nobody can play the piano on a stool like that. When

Andy graduated from high school he brought me this new one.

"Finally Andy started to play better, and once he started to play better he gained confidence in himself and you could see the changes. And then he *really* became interested. But when his interest peaked was when he could hear things coming together that he and I had worked on. His music had come to life. After he had been with me for about three years I began talking to him about going to school—to a conservatory. I had to push him out for his own growth. By then I was talking to his parents quite often on the phone, and I think I helped to get them off his back. I said things about him that they never knew, and they were always so surprised. I really reintroduced them to their son." In any case, Andy went to a conservatory in Boston for three years, and now, at twenty-three, is well launched on a music career as both a pianist and a teacher.

"But the student who really fascinated me," Mitchell says, "was a boy named Larry who came from a very poor Polish-American family in New Jersey. He had never been exposed to anything—he knew absolutely nothing. But he had talent like nobody I've ever seen. He can be any kind of pianist he wants to be. He had a job as a maintenance man at a factory in New Jersey, lifting heavy desks and furniture. The plant had a little auditorium with a piano, and after work he somehow taught himself to play on that piano. One of the executives heard him and asked who his teacher was. He said he had never had a lesson. The executive had heard Ruff and me in a concert at Dartmouth and he sent Larry to me. He was about twenty-two, and he was extremely crude. If you've seen stevedores and that kind of men who sit in a very macho and overbearing way, that's how he sat. He was like a street boy, knocking things around, and his feet were all over—he would have put them on top of the piano if I had let him. His hands were so calloused they felt like marble.

"That boy worked! I've never worked with anybody who kept someone busy the way he did. If you gave him two études to learn, he'd learn four; if you gave him four, he'd learn eight. He'd sneak into that company auditorium after everybody left and practice for hours. He came to me every Saturday at noon—at twelve o'clock the doorbell rang—and he didn't leave until six. And we never felt the time going by. When he first came to me he knew the keyboard and that's about all. He could read just enough to get the notes off the page into his ear, and he didn't know any chords. I taught him every chord he knows. But once he learned them he could juggle them like a master. He was also a great improviser, and he was equally at home with jazz and classical music. On Saturdays when I was waiting for him to come there was always an excitement in me because I knew how hard he had worked. It was just amazing what he had learned in a week.

"This went on for three years. Sometimes he'd call and say he couldn't come because he didn't have any money, and I'd tell him to come anyway. Finally I stopped him from coming. I took inventory of our work together and I realized that Saturday after Saturday, year after year, if I had a chance to go somewhere on a weekend I never did. I never would cancel him. And I realized that on Saturday nights I would be so spent—so tired and out of it—that I had to go to bed. I knew that he no longer needed me. He had found his direction and could go off on his own."

In Mitchell's teaching, a straight line isn't always the shortest distance to where he wants to go. "I guess I must ask the right questions," he says. "If somebody's playing in a certain way I can often pinpoint the problems, and they have nothing to do with playing the piano physically or what's going on in that room. I might say, 'Stop a moment—is everything all right? Did something happen to you this week?' And they will start to talk. As long as I can remember, people will tell me things they won't tell anyone else—in fact, they always seem to *want* me to know it. It's a lucky gift for a teacher to have because it frees students of so much.

"In the case of Larry, all that crudeness gradually disappeared. He had learned it from his peers—they all acted the same way—and yet deep within this boy was a desire to play the piano. He couldn't have discussed it with his peers or even with his parents. In the second year he cut off every one of those people, and he did it very nicely—he just started slipping away, being by himself, meeting new friends, coming to concerts in New York, which he had never done before. He had never seen Horowitz play, and I said 'You must go.' He got two tickets—one for his mother, who didn't have any interest in music—and when he next came to me he talked and talked about Horowitz and analyzed every aspect of that performance. And he never sat at the piano hunched over in that macho way again. From that day on he sat up straight."

Mitchell's method is to develop the material he is given, not to impose on his students some system of his own. They tell him where they want to go and he helps them to find the road. "But usually they wind up going in a different direction," he says. "I might play a phrase from a classical piece, for instance, and they say 'What was that?' Their ear makes them curious."

. . .

"Pianos are all so marvelous," Mitchell says, "and so different. You've got to acquaint yourself with them and you have to join personalities. There's a connection—a touch—that they insist you understand. The fun is to get together with the instrument."

Often, however, the piano wants no part of the fun. Not long ago Mitchell turned up in the late afternoon at a campus where he was to give an evening concert, and he went to look at the auditorium. What he found was a brand-new Steinway concert grand, as stiff as only a brand-new concert grand can be. He sat down and played scales for three hours straight, stopping only when the audience began to arrive. Then he played a full concert with Ruff. If he still hadn't quite joined personalities with the piano, he had at least made it more compliant. "These colleges get these new pianos and they're so proud of them," he says, "and they put them out on the stage and the piano says, 'Play me.' And you think, 'Why *me*? Let someone else play it.'"

Still, there are worse fates than having to play a good new piano, as every jazz pianist knows from years of playing bad old pianos. Of all Mitchell's encounters with bad pianos, however, he recalls only one with bitterness. In the early 1950s he and Ruff went to a black college in Montgomery, Alabama, and he was given a mediocre upright, though the college owned a decent concert grand. "The president didn't want to give us his best piano—he wanted to give us one that he felt was suitable for a jazz musician," Mitchell says. "Though the president was a black man he had no respect for the music we were going to play, which was black music. I pointed out that my contract stipulates a nine-foot grand for my concerts, but he wouldn't give in, and I refused to play. That's the only time I've ever refused to play."

The worst piano Mitchell remembers was at a poor black college in Arkansas where he and Ruff played many years ago. "They had moved this Wurlitzer fifty miles in the back of a truck and sat it up there on the stage and didn't tune it," he says. "We were late getting there, and I walked out on the stage, which had flowers on it and looked so nice, and I hit this thing and it did seventeen-tone scales. I couldn't do anything with it. I put my hand down on G and I was getting between G and A flat, or between G and F sharp, or between G and *any* thing but G. The water just started to pour out of me. But I had to play—all those people were sitting there in the audience. It was the quietest sort of response. Everybody knew something was wrong, but nobody knew what—except me. They were thinking, 'Does he really sound like that?'

"I learned long ago that it does no good to complain. Once you start complaining you're throwing yourself into another state. You think, 'This damn piano,' and you get mad at it, and when you get angry you play angry, and you can't project who *you* really are because you've been transformed into an angry person and you have all kinds of things going through your mind. Instead you say, 'What *does* it do? Will it do *any*thing? Let's check it out.' And you try to work with it, and sometimes it's a lot of fun because many pianos give you a different response from the one you're used to, and that makes you play differently."

Mitchell is acutely sensitive to the physical space that he plays in. "If I'm going to play anywhere," he says, "I start to prepare myself earlier in the day—even if I don't want to. It seems that I have nothing to do with it at all. Things start happening inside—your stomach starts it and then your whole body starts it. I begin to change into the person I am when I play the piano. I try to arrive at the hall about an hour beforehand to get the feel of the place. Every room is different. The way it looks, the vibrations, the decor, the people, the piano, where the piano is in relation to the audience—everything affects a player's playing. I look at people in the audience when I first go in because after I start to play I never see anybody. Just getting acquainted with the faces I'm going to play for has something to do with my performance."

No element varies more than the acoustics. "There are some halls that you feel you can't fill with sound—the acoustics are so bad," Mitchell says. "Those rooms make you want to work yourself to death because you just don't think you're being heard. Sometimes I can't hear Ruff, and he's standing right next to the piano. When I play the softest note I want it to reach every part of the hall. That's one of the nicest things about playing in college auditoriums in the United States in recent years; some thought has been given to the acoustics."

Nightclubs are the severest challenge. "The thing about playing in nightclubs that's so difficult for me," Mitchell says, "is to get over all the stuff going on around you that has to go on. The first thing is waitresses; if they don't sell any liquor they're not going to make any money. If the cash register doesn't ring, that means nobody's buying. You must get to the point where you don't hear that any more. You put yourself in another gear. Rooms can be quieted; you can turn nightclubs into concert halls. If you're really *on* you can make cash registers stop ringing and make bartenders stand still. But you have to draw on every ounce of spiritual energy you have. Ultimately you assert your authority, and people respond to strength. It's not really *your* authority. That authority is coming straight from the spirit. The spirit is being kind to you and letting you make it."

• • •

One morning in May of 1983, Mitchell got a call from

Dunedin telling him that his father had been taken to the hospital with a heart attack. As soon as Mitchell hung up the phone he knew that his father was dying, and he caught a midday plane to Florida. His father died the next day.

I thought of the oppressive weight that the father had exerted on the son for so many years, and I wondered how Mitchell would be affected by the sudden release. I didn't find out until September. Mitchell was gone for four months, and the man who came back to New York was not the same man who had gone away. He hadn't done anything all summer—he hadn't even touched a piano—and he wasn't in good shape.

"When I got to that hospital and saw my father," he said, "I never thought I'd be so *pained*. I never knew that inside myself I had another slot; I thought I knew all about pain. I never realized until then that my father and I were as close as we were and that we had never said that to each other. At first all these flashbacks went through my mind—about how he treated me. But then I thought about *his* life as a man, and where he came from, and how he was raised. His early life was very difficult. He came from a family that had to farm and his people were extremely poor. He ran away from home—all the kids did—because he wanted to better himself.

"After he died I realized that he understood something about me that *I* had never understood, which was that I might have become very wild—I mean really *out*—if I hadn't been kept under a certain amount of discipline. I think he recognized something in me that was unlike anybody in our family, and I guess he was trying to control forces that could have been detrimental to me if I'd been given the freedom to do all the crazy things that occurred to me. Like the time I took that train to New York when I was eleven. Ever since I was a child he put his foot down on my neck all the time. It was always 'Don't, don't, don't, don't, don't,' and I was always 'Do, do, do, do, do.' But maybe he just didn't know the right way to do what he thought he had to do. Emotionally he wasn't a man who showed what he felt. I never once heard him say to me that I played the piano well. The only comment about my music he ever made was after one of my concerts in New Haven. He said, 'Don't play so hard.' He would come here to my apartment in New York, and I'd practice, and he'd sit perfectly quiet with his eyes closed, and when I finished he never said a word. He just sat.

"Well, at the time of his funeral I met a lot of his friends, and those old men told me how my father talked about me. One of them said, 'You know, your dad said you were his heart. He said that you could really do no wrong.' I couldn't believe it. I said, 'My daddy said that?' Another man said, 'Your daddy thought you were the best piano player in the world.' It was so strange to hear that coming from someone else. My biggest regret is that we weren't able to talk to each other in an open, emotional way—to say who we really were. He was too proud for that. When I was with him it was always 'I'm the father and you're the son.'

"He was a fine man and he meant well. I always knew there was nothing he wouldn't do for me. I've been in music all my life and I've never taken any guff from anybody because I didn't have to. Somehow I knew that if anything happened to me my father would straighten it out. In my mind he was always that kind of person. I knew he was always there. When he died, my life changed. I realized that I had been a child—that all of my life I had never really grown up. Now I feel very strongly that I must carry on all the things that he started."

Mitchell was shaken by the discovery of how deeply he and his father loved each other. "I was numb for four months," he said. "I couldn't move. Things were shifting in me, and I could feel the changes. But they were all for the better. I found out a lot of things about myself, especially in relation to how I played the piano. I've gone into another gear since my father died. As I started to reflect, I started to relax. Ordinarily I'm at my most tense when I play the piano because it's a matter of grabbing inside, and pulling, and giving. But now I've learned that I can do all this with a totally relaxed body because I was told things about my father and how he felt about me. All the tensions I've carried inside me since I was a child are gone. I feel that I've been given something. I think what I've been given is all the good things I really knew about my dad, and all the other things have just disappeared."

. . .

If the spirit is kind to Mitchell, it's because he trusts it and feels that he is its servant. Often in a concert he reaches a high that borders on a religious experience. He enters a trance-like state, expending prodigious energy at the key-board and feeling no fatigue at the end. "You try to cross over," he says, "into that part of you that's always there but is only alive when you're playing."

On such occasions the audience knows it is in the presence of a mystery. "When you sit down at that instrument," Mitchell says, "you owe it to yourself, you owe it to your audience, you owe it to the spirit, to transform yourself into nothing else but you and that instrument. The world is totally shut out. There is something about you and that instrument that now is the purest time in your life. It's always like a first time, being purified. With all the madnesses of the world going on, you cannot think of anything else except that you are sitting at this piano, and this piano and you are together, and now, 'Let's go!' Because when you are really playing well you are in almost uncontrolled happiness. People can see you doing it, and they can feel it, but nobody knows that inside you it's the happiest you've ever been in your life."

7 . . . Venice

One day in July of 1983, I happened to call Willie Ruff and he mentioned that he was about to go to Italy for a few weeks. I assumed that he was going for a vacation, or to see friends, or to practice his Italian—the usual reasons. But then I remembered that with Ruff there are no usual reasons, and I asked him the purpose of his trip.

"I'm going to Venice to play Gregorian chants on my French horn in St. Mark's cathedral at night when nobody else is there," he said. "I'll take my tape recorder along and make a tape of what I play."

That was a sound I knew I would like to hear and a sight I would like to see. But why Venice?

"Venice was the center of the musical world in the 1500s and 1600s," Ruff said, "and that was mainly because of the remarkable acoustics in St. Mark's. It's where a very important style of polyphonic music began. The great innovative composers of the period were Venetians—the Gabrielis, Zarlino, Monteverdi—and what inspired them was this church that gave incredible richness and clarity to what they wrote. I want to know what that sound is like."

I asked Ruff how the idea of making this pilgrimage had come to him.

"It goes back to my student days at Yale," he said, "when I studied with Paul Hindemith. Hindemith had totally immersed himself in the history of music, and he insisted that students coming to work with him do the same. He introduced us to all this fabulous music that had come out of Venice and he made us see what a crucial bridge it was to everything that followed. He was also deeply interested in the history of science. He talked very forcefully in his lectures about the scientists of the old world who got involved in music theory—especially Johannes Kepler, who was his hero. He spent twenty years writing an opera about Kepler's life. He said that if Kepler hadn't been a musical theorist as well as a mathematician he might not have discovered the three laws of planetary motion that are still milestones in the natural sciences."

I already knew about the Hindemith–Kepler connection. At Yale I had heard Ruff talk about how Hindemith excited him with Kepler's "music of the spheres"—the theory that musical principles are involved in the paths that the planets take around the sun. In 1619, in a book called *The Harmony of the World,* Kepler described the consonances that the orbiting planets would make, but there was no way to test the theory. With the advent of the computer, however, Ruff saw a way to bring the music of the spheres down to earth. In 1978 he enlisted the help of an eminent Yale geologist, Professor John Rodgers, and they fed formulas into a computer-synthesizer instructing it to generate the frequencies that Kepler published. The resulting LP record of Kepler's "music," widely reported in the press, has since sold thousands of copies to science buffs everywhere, especially in Japan. Ruff mails them out from the Yale post office and puts the proceeds into the Duke Ellington fellowships.

Now, as Ruff talked about Hindemith and the acoustics in St. Mark's, the rest of the connection was falling into place, and I saw what was drawing him there. I asked if I could join him. He reminded me that he didn't have permission to play in St. Mark's and didn't know if he could get it. I reminded him that he didn't have any assurance when we left for Shanghai that he and Mitchell would be allowed to play in China; I would take my chances. Ruff said he hoped to reach Venice in about a week. I said I'd meet him there.

. . .

I was in Italy during World War II and have been back many times since. Of all foreign countries it's the one I know best. But Venice to me is a different country altogether—an Eastern place, perched so far out on Italy's eastern rim that it has slid into the water. I still remember my surprise as a soldier when I first saw the gaudy striped cathedrals of Pisa and Siena, with their playful colors and glittering gold mosaics. How had such exotic notions pushed their way into the pious architecture of Tuscany? "Byzantine," the guides said. "Trade routes from the East," they said. "From Venice," they said. After the war, when I finally got to Venice and saw

St. Mark's basilica and its five Byzantine domes, I felt no kinship with the Italy I knew. Something old and mysterious was at work there.

Only once did I feel that I was in touch with the city, and that was when I was leaving it by boat. I had always wanted to visit Jerusalem, and it was important to me to approach the Holy Land by sea, slowly and with some preparation. I didn't want to get into a jet plane in New York and wake up in Israel. Rummaging in the travel ads, I found a car ferry that left Venice on Wednesday evening and reached Haifa on Sunday morning, stopping at Piraeus and Limassol. That was the boat for me. I had first seen the Mediterranean from North Africa, when I was stationed in Algiers and Oran, and I have loved Mediterranean ports ever since for their ancient mixture of races. A car ferry to Israel was therefore the answer to many old stirrings, and on that Wednesday evening, just before sunset, as my boat sailed out into the Adriatic past Venice, the crazy city finally made sense to me. It was a creature of the Levant, and that was where I was going.

Now, in 1983, I was back, bringing emotional baggage of my own to my rendezvous with Ruff. I had cabled him the name of the hotel where I would be staying, and when I checked in I asked if there was a message for me. The concierge brightened.

"You should call Mister Willie," he said, handing me a piece of paper with a number on it. I did, and got Ruff, and he came over and we found a table overlooking the Grand Canal where we could eat and talk. Again, it was almost sundown. Ruff chatted with the waiter in fluent Italian. He had been in Venice almost two days, he said, and he already knew his way around the convoluted streets and canals. He had also spent some time in St. Mark's, getting the feel of the place, and he was eager to tell me about it. But first I had to know more about the various forces that had gone into his being here now.

"In my first year as a music student at Yale," Ruff recalled, "I was required to take a very boring history-of-music course. We were taught all about the Catholic church service, and being an Alabama Baptist I wasn't too interested in that. The professor was one of those teachers who never tell you *why* you're being made to study something. He made us learn all the old liturgical modes from a book called the *Liber Usualis* and translate them into modern notation. Later, of course, that turned out to be very valuable because those modes were so central to how Europe developed its secular harmony. But I had no inkling of their importance at the time.

"In my second year I was allowed to sign up for a course with Hindemith, and it was on the history of the theory of music. After that introductory course I never wanted to hear another word about the history of music. But Hindemith was my whole reason for being at Yale. Back in Columbus I had seen an interview with Charlie Parker in which he was asked, 'If you could take a year and do anything at all, how would you spend the year?' He said there was a cat at Yale named Paul Hindemith and that he'd like to go and work with him. Hindemith's music was becoming known to innovative jazzmen, especially his *Symphonic Metamorphosis on Themes by Weber,* which has a strong jazz flavoring. His own instrument was the viola, but he had supported himself by playing drums in a jazz band in hotels all over Europe before coming to the United States in 1939. Anyway, what Charlie Parker said stuck with me, and when my horn teacher in Columbus, Abe Kniaz, also insisted that I go to Yale so I could study with Hindemith, that settled it."

Ruff recalls Hindemith as a short, round, bald man who was jovial when he was pleased—a condition that evidently didn't occur often. "He'd get angry if you performed sloppily and he'd swear at you in German and throw things at you," Ruff said. "I remember he emptied a music stand at one trumpet player. He threw every item at him, one by one —every sheet of music, the pencil, and the stand itself. Just ran him off the stage."

But when Hindemith taught the history of music, Ruff forgot that he hated the history of music. "He made it *live,*" Ruff said. "He was a nut on the necessity for the person who was going to make music his life—not his living; his *life*— to be in touch with the musical past that made the present possible. The way he did it was to make us experience old music by performing it. He wanted us to actually *hear* it. He would organize programs of very early music, and those of us who were in his class had to play it and sing it. If the old instruments were still available, like the krumhorn and the sackbut, we'd use those.

"The music of St. Mark's was central to what Hindemith

was trying to teach us. It also turned out to be the music that spoke most directly to me, maybe because of the luxurious sound that Andrea and Giovanni Gabrieli achieved in their polychoral compositions." The Gabrielis, uncle and nephew, successively dominated the music of Venice in the late 1500s, giving the city a renown as the center of European music that lasted well into the Baroque era, perpetuated by such composers as Monteverdi and Vivaldi. The Gabrielis wrote for vast choirs of voices and instruments, which sang and played antiphonally from opposite lofts of St. Mark's cathedral. Hindemith, knowing that the acoustics of St. Mark's had inspired the Gabrielis to reach for such remarkable effects, tried to approximate the sound by having his class sing and play the Gabrielis' music from the balconies of Sprague Hall, one of Yale's music auditoriums. Once he even took Ruff's class to New York to play in the huge entrance hall of the Metropolitan Museum of Art.

"When we played that music of the Venetian school," Ruff said, "it moved me harmonically, and rhythmically it thrilled me to my roots. Under Hindemith's direction it had none of that tight-assed, choirmaster, metronome strictness. It was performed with the kind of rhythmic abandon that's common in the jazz world. What Hindemith did was to make me know that I had to discard nothing of my own cultural past. I've had a fascination with that music ever since. I knew that someday I wanted to play it in a place that was architecturally interesting and that also had some connection with the music I'm involved with now."

That connection was revealed to Ruff when he came upon a recording of a concert that Paul Robeson had given at Carnegie Hall in 1958. Robeson, who could sing folk songs in many languages, demonstrated that the folk music of widely disparate countries comes from a common source. He sang an American Negro spiritual, an East African tribal chant, a thirteenth-century plain chant from Czechoslovakia and an old Jewish chant from the Near East that were strikingly similar. "I had known that American spirituals were a source of wonder in Europe when they were first performed there by touring choirs like the Fisk Jubilee Singers," Ruff said. "They were just close enough to the Europeans' own folk songs and to their religious music to be strangely familiar.

"Robeson's point was that it all ties in—that the folk music of huge areas of the world is compatible. And he asked, 'Why is this so?' He said it was because the Abyssinian church and the church of the Sudan were a part of the Eastern church of Byzantium. Therefore, music from many parts of Africa and the Near East found its way into the liturgy of the early Byzantine church and subsequently filtered out into Europe."

There it has popped up in odd pockets ever since, often to the surprise of its discoverers. It was the folk music that Béla Bartók and Zoltán Kodály found, for instance, when they went to remote villages of Hungary and Czechoslovakia in the early 1900s to collect peasant songs—and that Bartók later incorporated so vividly in his own work. The songs were based on old Greek ecclesiastical modes and on pentatonic scales from Central Asia, which, Bartók said, freed him from "the tyrannical rule of the major and minor keys." Thus Bartók was listening to Slovakian plain chants long before Robeson picked up the trail from another direction, and now Ruff had picked it up from Robeson.

"Suddenly it hit me," he said, "that what I wanted to do was to play my horn in St. Mark's. But what would I play? I realized that I'd have to go back to the *Liber Usualis,* the book that I couldn't wait to sell after my first year at Yale. So I took it out of the Yale music library and started learning the material again. *Liber Usualis* means 'the book of use,' referring to the hymns and chants that have been most used in the Catholic liturgy. These in turn were colored by the music of the Byzantine church. So what I'll be playing in St. Mark's is sacred music that goes back to the Middle Ages and that fits directly into this church. That whole stream of music came through here and was waiting for the Venetian masters to develop it. Those sacred chants are also at the core of my spirituals, as Robeson made me realize, so I'm going to play some of them, too."

Before coming to Venice, Ruff had stopped off in Rome. He attended an early Sunday morning Mass in St. Peter's and a later one in Santa Maria Maggiore, taping the Gregorian chants in those two historic churches because he wanted to know how they are used in the liturgy today. Then he went on to Venice, where he had never been before.

"As soon as I got off the *vaporetto,*" he said, "I felt that this was where I should be." He checked into his hotel and went around to see St. Mark's before it closed. "The place was full of tourists," Ruff said, "and I walked around clapping my hands to test the echoes while everyone else was looking at the mosaics. There are five enormous domes— and domes are interesting musically. What is it that's so *balanced* in that church? Today I went back and just sat and looked and listened. I eavesdropped on the different sightseeing tours, trying to hear what the guides were saying about the church's history. I heard tours in English, German, Spanish, French, Italian and Portuguese, and not one of the guides mentioned one word about the music. Everybody in St. Mark's was on a visual trip. I was the only person there who was listening for a distant sound."

. . .

The next morning Ruff set out on his mission systematically. His first goal was to get permission to play in St. Mark's. He had consulted various Catholic scholars before leaving the United States, and they agreed that a sum in the neighborhood of 50,000 lire, or forty dollars, would probably be persuasive. One of them, a student of canon law, said that the proper word to use in such a transaction was *offerta*. Ruff also had a letter from Yale University attesting that he was a member of the faculty on a scholarly quest.

Ruff's second goal was to study the acoustics of Venice's other churches before playing in St. Mark's. "I want to visit as many as I can in the next few days," he said, "and play some Gregorian chants on my horn when nobody else is there. Otherwise I won't have any basis of comparison. All I know is that St. Mark's is different from the other churches here. What I need to know is *how*."

Thus primed for the day's conquests, we went forth into the city. Even in midmorning St. Mark's square had no shortage of its two main commodities: tourists and pigeons. If Venice is sinking, it is not from the weight of time but from the weight of sightseers. We walked across the vast piazza toward the bulky presence of St. Mark's cathedral, anchoring the square at its eastern end, as it has since 1067. We joined the throngs pushing their way in. (During the summer, 25,000 tourists a day enter the church.)

I stood in the nave and looked up at the huge domes, thinking of them for the first time as hollowed space, conducive to sound. The five domes form a Greek cross—three over the nave and one over each transept. Ruff had told me that music hates opposite walls and 90-degree angles. St. Mark's, I now saw, was a temple of rounded surfaces—not only the domes, but the Romanesque arches that they rest on and that also frame the upper balconies, where the Gabrielis placed their antiphonal choirs.

Ruff asked a guard if he could talk to someone connected with the church, and we were led through several dark corridors to the office of a monsignor. He was a suave, silver-haired man who had the look of Venetian nobility. He also had the look of someone who was adroit at his job of screening petitioners and turning them away. Ruff seemed nervous—not sure that his Italian was good enough to explain the complexities of his project. "I hope he speaks English," he said to me.

The monsignor greeted Ruff with a politeness that was neither warm nor cold and waited for him to state his business. Ruff began by introducing himself. (The conversation had just enough fragments of familiar Italian so that I could piece it together.) Ruff presented his elegant letter from Yale with its university seal. The monsignor said he didn't speak English and handed the letter back. Ruff pressed on, extolling the musical glories of Venice. I heard the sonorous words *acustica* and *armonica* and *eco* and *Gabrieli*. The monsignor seemed unmoved by the musical glories of Venice. He asked Ruff how he proposed to study the acoustics of St. Mark's. Ruff said he wanted to play his French horn in the balconies and in the nave. Fine, the monsignor said. Go ahead. Play. Ruff said he meant that he wanted to play alone, at night, when the church wasn't full of people. The monsignor shrugged. It was the Latin shrug that needs no translating. He said he couldn't give permission for such a request. Ruff asked who *could* give permission. The monsignor shrugged again, his hands spread wide in the classic position of helplessness. He said maybe the *arcidiacono*. The strange word fell into our midst like a stone. Ruff asked if he meant the archdiocese, and what city was that in? Where would he have to go? Rome? Milan? But the interview was suddenly over and we were back out in the corridor, and then we were back out in St. Mark's square, blinking in the bright Mediterranean sun. "I never even got to mention the *offerta*," Ruff said.

Ruff didn't waste any time bemoaning his fate. He had been given one word—*arcidiacono*—and that was enough. Now he was eager to get started on his next project: playing in Venice's other churches. He had made a list of them, and for his first test he selected a church called San Rocco, on the other side of the Grand Canal, which he had heard was quite deserted. We walked to his hotel to get his horn and then made our way through a maze of alleys to San Rocco, Ruff moving with the agility of a native son.

At the church, his research turned out to be correct. Only two or three people were in the nave, and they were finishing their prayers and would soon be gone. Ruff told me he would wait until the church was empty—he didn't want to disturb or offend anyone. Meanwhile he got out his *Liber Usualis* and opened it to a hymn called the "Pange Lingua," which he said was one of the oldest and most beautiful melodies in the book. Finally the last worshiper left. San Rocco was absolutely still.

Ruff lifted his French horn to his mouth and blew what was at the most a sixteenth note. It was stopped by an old sacristan who came running at high speed, shouting *"Vietato! Vietato!"* and repeatedly extending his arms in the motion of a baseball umpire signifying that a runner is safe. He stood in front of Ruff, a small man, barely five feet tall, shaking with outrage. *"Chiesa! Chiesa!"* he shouted, meaning that we were in a church. "This is church music," Ruff said. He couldn't believe what was happening. The old man had struck like a summer squall. Ruff showed him his *Liber Usualis,* a black book that looks like a Bible and has the solemn weight of Roman Catholic authority. He flicked through the pages, stopping to point out the "Gloria" and various other chants that are still used in the liturgy today. The sacristan was in no mood for ecclesiastical proofs. This was a *chiesa* and there was to be no music.

Ruff made one more start at protesting his good intentions, but in midsentence the humor of his situation hit him. Ruff and Mitchell are both men of tremendous humor, quick to laugh; once, on a concert tour in Europe, they got laughing so hard in a hotel lobby that the manager ordered them to check out immediately and never come back. Now Ruff hardly made it to the door, and when he was out on the steps of San Rocco he doubled up. "That's got to be the shortest note anybody ever played," he said. "I had just finished my inhale and was about to blow out when I saw this flash coming at me out of the corner of my eye—at the velocity of Jesse Owens. It was the fastest putdown of my career."

But the encounter drained some of Ruff's optimism. "If that's a typical reception by the clergy," he said, "I think my preliminary tests are over." He wanted to try once more—in a church called the Frari, which was right around the corner. Inside, one look told us that it was no place to play the French horn. Not only was the church quite full of tourists. Architecturally it was an immense Gothic barn, with none of the enveloping curves of St. Mark's; any music performed there might quickly dissipate. One look would also have told the Gabrielis to go somewhere else with their antiphonal choirs.

Artistically, however, the Frari rewarded us with Titian's *Assumption* over the altar—a giant painting that almost vibrated with color and motion—and to the left of the altar we came upon a chapel that contained the tomb of Monteverdi. Someone had left a small bunch of flowers on it that were beginning to wilt. Ruff was moved by the tomb. "I wish I could play for *him*," Ruff said. He looked around the crowded church and thought better of it. But the moment seemed to give him an idea, and when we got out in the street it had taken shape.

"You know, Stravinsky is buried in Venice," Ruff said. "There's an island called San Michele that's the cemetery for the whole city, and it has one section of Russian Orthodox graves." I remembered seeing a television documentary about Stravinsky after he died in 1971 that ended with his coffin being taken by boat across the waters of Venice. "*That's* who I can play for," Ruff said. "Come on. I'm going to play the 'Pange Lingua' for Stravinsky."

We walked to the Grand Canal and caught the *vaporetto* that takes passengers out to San Michele and several other islands. It left the main city and headed across a strait of open water, and I thought the cemetery might be quite far away. But the ride took only ten minutes. On the way I asked Ruff why Stravinsky was such a giant to jazz musicians.

"He's *the* giant," Ruff said. "He was so advanced and hip. He's the main hero to jazz musicians because he was *weird*. That was an important word in the bebop era, and it was highly complimentary. It meant that you were thinking with superintelligence and that you were pushing beyond the conventions. At the end of World War II the first cadre of highly educated black people was coming into the mainstream of American society. These people needed a music—a music that was more of their day. The sophistication of jazz as it existed then was not enough. There was nobody, not even Duke Ellington, who was speaking to that period as these people needed to be spoken to musically. But Stravinsky spoke to them: first to Charlie Parker and Dizzy Gillespie and Thelonious Monk and Art Blakey and Kenny Clarke and Max Roach—the great bebop innovators in New York who pulled all this music together. Then the music was taken in an even more outrageous direction by Miles Davis and John Coltrane and the other pioneers of 'modern jazz.' Stravinsky was a god to them all. He's what modern jazz was all about."

We got off at the cemetery and the custodian gave us a map of the grounds. Probably he thought we had come to see Ezra Pound. We took a gravel path leading past rows of tall cypresses that were the only touch of formal landscaping. Four gravediggers were singing at their work, and Ruff found this encouraging; here at least, among the dead, there was no objection to music. The graves were long slabs lying on the ground, not upright headstones in the American and English style. We found Stravinsky and his compatriots in a small enclave at a far end of the cemetery. His immediate neighbor was Aspasia, Widow of H.M. Alexander I, King of the Hellenes, and a few yards beyond that was a grave marked "SERGE DIAGHILEV, 1872–1929." That the impresario of *The Firebird, Petrouchka* and *The Rite of Spring* had preceded his composer to this distant plot of Mediterranean earth so long ago was one of the most touching of the Byzantine mysteries that kept being revealed to me.

Stravinsky's grave was a slab of white marble with just two words in slanted capital letters: IGOR STRAVINSKY. The letters were made of deep-blue stone embedded in the marble. They had the informal rhythm of calligraphy, the second *S* more antic than the first. "It looks like him," Ruff said; he was reminded of the graceful pen strokes on Stravinsky's own music manuscripts.

Ruff opened his *Liber Usualis* to the "Pange Lingua," took his horn out of its case, and looked around to see if he would be disturbing anyone. Only a few birds were within disturbing range, but Ruff was taking no chances and, as an afterthought, he put a mute in his horn. Then he stood by Stravinsky's grave and played. The ancient melody had great power, yet it also had a quality that was modern in its associations. Ruff looked quizzical, surprised by the same paradox, and when he finished he said, "Did you hear it? It was the mute! It never occurred to me when I put it in, but of course that was one of Stravinsky's favorite sounds. There are whole sections of *The Firebird* and *Petrouchka* that are scored specifically for muted horns and brasses. He was a master of that coloring—he could paint pictures with muted brass. It all came back to me when I started to play. I remembered how I went to *Fantasia* every night at our army base just to hear that sound. And how we used to play Stravinsky records over and over in the dayroom at Lockbourne. That sound is unique. If I had thought about it all morning I couldn't have come up with anything more distinctive— because it's also in Stravinsky's religious music. He wrote a number of Masses—he was rooted in the music of the liturgy."

Ruff played the "Pange Lingua" one more time, giving it a joyful lilt. Then he took the mute out of the horn and put the horn back in its case and we walked out of the cemetery and took the *vaporetto* back to Venice. Ruff was at ease. The frustrations of the morning had been blown away.

• • •

We got off the boat at St. Mark's square, and as we made our way past a row of bookstalls Ruff noticed a poster announcing that the Amherst College glee club was scheduled to sing in St. Mark's cathedral on the following Sunday. "Someone gave *them* permission," he said. "There must be somebody in charge of making special arrangements for that church. I'm going to find him." It was now midafternoon and the crowds milling around the entrance of St. Mark's were thick, but we joined them and let the gravitational force of tourism pull us into the basilica.

Ruff walked past the clusters of tour groups looking up at the mosaics that their guides were describing and went to the velvet rope at the rear of the church that partitioned off the chancel. Several sacristans were coming and going around the altar, and Ruff studied them for a while. Finally he said, "That's my man—I can work with him." Ruff's man was a genial middle-aged Italian, who said he was the *capo,* or chief, of the sacristans. Ruff went into his speech, and this time it went better than it had with the monsignor; he was more confident, and when he had finished praising the acoustics and the Gabrielis and explained that he wanted to play his horn there, the sacristan became almost as enthusiastic as Ruff. He said that Ruff should talk to the *arcidiacono.*

"Where is he?" Ruff asked.

"He's here in Venice," the sacristan said. "His name is Monsignor Spavento and his responsibility is for what happens in this church. In English I think you call him the archdeacon." So that was the dreaded *arcidiacono*—a mere mortal, like the Wizard of Oz. Earlier, the word had been thrown at us so fast that we hadn't stopped to analyze it and demystify it.

"How can I find him?" Ruff asked.

"He usually comes to the church around six o'clock at night," the sacristan said. "He will be here tomorrow. Can you come back then? I will take you to him."

"I'll be here," Ruff said.

That gave Ruff an empty day, and he had two pet projects to fill it with. In the morning he went to the town of Castelfranco to see a tailor who is known for the suits that he makes for musicians for their concert appearances. Ruff is a natty and eclectic dresser, and his wardrobe of elegant duds, cut by tailors that he has found as far away as Bali, needed replenishing. In the afternoon he went to an old library in Venice called the Biblioteca Nationale Marciana. He had a list of five Italian Renaissance composers whose manuscripts, now very scarce, he hoped to turn up for the Yale School of Music—especially the work of Carlo Gesualdo. In fact, as Ruff explained his quest I realized that Gesualdo was one of his major heroes.

"Gesualdo was the Thelonious Monk of his day," Ruff said. "He was the father of dissonance, and I'm amazed that he was able to stay alive and flourish because he must have offended everybody. He was so daring! Being introduced to him in a course on old music that was taught by a modern master like Hindemith was a thrill I've never forgotten, because here was a statement, made almost four hundred years earlier, that this man knew all about dissonance—about this rubbing together of notes." At the library Ruff unearthed six books of Gesualdo's *Canzoni,* five-part madrigals that scholars still marvel at for their audacity. He arranged to have them microfilmed and sent to New Haven. "It was like found gold," he said.

So the day was spent on the trail of new clothes and old music, and it was just on the hour of six—struck by the famous mechanical bell ringers of St. Mark's on their famous outdoor clock—when we got to the cathedral for Ruff's meeting with the *arcidiacono.* I told him I would wait for him at one of the outdoor cafés in St. Mark's square; this was one occasion when I thought he should present himself as a single pilgrim.

I found a table and settled down. The heat was ebbing out of the day, and the tables had begun to fill up with tourists released from their sightseeing vows and eager to restore their depleted energies. St. Mark's square has been called the world's biggest living room, and the string orchestras at the cafés struck up their medleys of Strauss waltzes and international hits like "Volare" that evoke memories of every European hotel and assure the tired traveler that the verities are intact. The major chords and saccharine violins lulled me into a world far simpler than the one that Ruff had been leading me through and that he was now trying, one last time, to conquer. I put him out of my mind and sank into the hot bath of "Tales from the Vienna Woods."

Ruff was gone a long time. Finally I saw him coming across the square. He was walking slowly and thoughtfully. He didn't look elated, but he also didn't look discouraged, and when he pulled up a chair I sensed that something more important than victory or defeat had happened to him.

"I found the sacristan," Ruff said, "and he took me to the rear of the church and led me to a confession booth. He tugged at the curtain and pulled it aside and I saw a very old priest slumped down in the seat—asleep. The sacristan tapped him and he woke up. He had white hair and a very old face and his tongue was working in that rhythmic way of people who have had a stroke. I thought, 'That finishes me. I'm dead.' But I started my speech anyway. By now I had it pretty well mastered, and I spoke with great feeling about my reverence for the magnificent music that had been created in St. Mark's, and about its place in the history of the music of Western civilization, and about the contribution of the

Gabrielis, and Monteverdi, and Zarlino, who was the most brilliant musical theorist of his day and had been *maestro di cappella* at St. Mark's, and I finally said that there must be something special about the acoustics, for all these achievements to have taken place in this basilica and not in any of Venice's other churches.

"Well, the monsignor started to come up out of his chair and I saw twenty-five years drop off this man's face and body. He sat up straight, and he became an elegant old man, and his tongue stopped working and his eyes opened wide and he said, 'The acoustics in St. Mark's are *perfetto!! Per-fet-to!*' I told him how I had heard all the tour guides in St. Mark's describing the marvels for the eye, but that for the marvels of the ear there didn't seem to be any memory or any monument. 'Is music really so perishable?' I asked. He looked at me harder. I had the feeling that he had been sitting and waiting there for years and nobody had ever come and talked to him about his church. He began to speak to me about the Byzantine consciousness that had gone into St. Mark's and about the distinctive style of the architecture and the mosaics. But then he remembered that my concern was with the acoustics, and he came back to that. He made it a dialogue. At one point I was struggling to express one of my ideas, and I said, 'Monsignor, I'm so sorry I have to make this request in my poor Italian,' and he stopped me and said, 'No, no! Don't apologize! I wish I could speak as much English as you speak Italian,' and he reached out and took both of my hands in his. I had expected this old man to be cold, but it was the warmest physical contact I think I've ever had. He continued to hold my hands in a very strong grip and he said, 'What do you want to do?'

"I told him I needed time to bring a microphone and a tape recorder into the church and that I wanted to take some measurements for the qualities of the sound, which I would do by using a musical instrument. He asked me what instrument I would use, and I told him I was a *cornista,* and he said *'Bene!'* I said I wanted to go to different parts of the basilica and just walk around and play, but that I needed silence. He said, 'How much time?' I didn't want to press my luck, so I said, 'An hour and a half; two hours maximum.' He said, 'Would tomorrow night be all right?' I said it would be wonderful. He said that a side chapel of the church stayed open for a Mass until seven-thirty, but if I would come to the side door at that time the sacristan would let me in and I could stay until nine-thirty.

"I thanked him and started to leave, but he held me. He said, 'Tell me, are you Latin American?' I had noticed him studying my face; he hadn't seen many like me. I said, 'No sir, I'm an American—I'm a mixture of American and African.' He said, 'You are an *Afro*-American?' Well, that's not a word I often use, but I said, 'Yes, sir, I am an Afro-American.' He said, 'This is the first time I have ever talked to an *Afro*-American.' He was still holding me in that warm grip. Suddenly he said, 'The Mediterranean! That's where the civilization of the West came from. That's what brought together this rich mixture of cultures from Africa and many other regions. That's what makes this church unique. St. Mark's itself is this mixture?' Then he said, 'What an idea! Wouldn't it be something if the glorious musical history of this church were to be brought back to the attention of the world by an *Afro*-American?'"

. . .

The next morning Ruff spent an hour in St. Mark's, learning his way around. He wanted to know how to reach the balconies and lofts, and he scrambled up and down the different flights of stairs. In the afternoon, like an athlete preparing for a big match, he went back to his hotel to rest. At seven-thirty we went to the side door of the church; the people who had attended Mass were just coming out. The sacristan was waiting for us, and he led us into the vast basilica. We were the only people there.

Ruff set up a camera tripod in the middle of the nave and put a microphone where the camera would ordinarily be. From there he ran a wire to his tape recorder, which he placed on the floor next to the tripod. It was a small monaural recorder; Ruff wasn't after stereophonic sound, which he considers a distortion. People's ears are so close together, he says, that they receive sound in a way that is more monaural than stereophonic. The encircling music of a Sony Walkman may be an acoustical treat, but it's not how music is really heard.

Ruff turned the tape recorder on, checked to make sure that it was going, picked up his French horn and blew one

note, a concert C, not particularly loud. The note filled the
entire church. It was a note of amazing volume and purity,
one that seemed to seek out every inch of the basilica and
leave no crevice unoccupied. If Ruff had played only that one
note his trip would have made its point; the acoustics were
indeed *perfetto*. Ruff then walked around the nave, stopping
under each of the five domes to blow a few notes. He always
announced where he was ("I'm standing under the main
dome, facing the congregation"); the teacher in him saw to
that. I thought of all the students who would listen to his
tape and hear, however remotely, what the Gabrielis heard.

Next Ruff climbed to the balcony over the main entrance
and played from there. Then he went to the side lofts and
played. Wherever he went, the music filled the church; distance didn't attenuate the sound. Then he came back down
and checked the tape by playing part of it back. "That's it!"
he said. "That's what my horn sounds like. It's never been
caught before."

That was the end of the preliminaries. Ruff propped up
his *Liber Usualis* on a small altar halfway down the aisle and
started to play Gregorian chants. The first was the Gloria
from Mass no. 2; the second was the Kyrie from Mass no. 8.
Both of them were jubilant melodies, nothing like the lugubri-
ous minor hymns that I associated with Catholic services. I
sat across the nave from Ruff, watching the changes as the
church settled down for the night. The last sunlight picked
up the gold in the high mosaics around the dome nearest the
main entrance; then, abruptly, all color was gone from the

basilica and I saw it as a skeleton—as the building that the builders built, without ornamentation. The five domes now looked enormous. Outside, the mechanical bell ringers struck a quarter-hour, and once, when Ruff paused between Gregorian chants, the merry strains of Offenbach drifted in from the square.

Ruff played an Agnus Dei and I was in the world's biggest sound chamber, wrapped in music. "It doesn't take any breath," Ruff said. "I could play forever." He played the Gloria from Mass no. 8, and the sacristan appeared from wherever he had been. "Gloria," he said, wanting to tell us that he knew it; it's still part of his liturgy. Seeing that Ruff was now in partial darkness, he lit a candle and put it on the altar next to the *Liber Usualis.* Then he left again. I moved to another part of the nave, and when Ruff played a Sanctus I noticed how extraordinarily long the echo was—about six seconds. The successive notes lingered in the air and joined to form chords. With such acoustics, I thought, the Gabrielis could hardly miss. St. Mark's was telling them how to write polyphonic music.

Next Ruff played the "Pange Lingua," without the mute that he had used so as not to waken the dead at Stravinsky's cemetery. The unmuted melody asserted its ancient authority, as it presumably had in that church since the Middle Ages, though perhaps no two people had ever listened to it as intently, there being no other sight or sound in the basilica. It had been emptied of distraction; Ruff and I were alone with our emotions. When he finished the "Pange Lingua" I wasn't looking in his direction, and the next music I heard was so unexpected that it sent a chill through me. It was the "Pange Lingua" again, but it seemed to be sung in a woman's voice. I walked over near Ruff; the sound was coming from his horn, but he was playing very quietly, and what was filling the church was one of the purest contraltos I have ever heard. When he stopped I told him about it. "I was thinking about Miss Celia," Ruff said. He meant Celia Appleton, the singer in the Baptist church in Sheffield, whose voice had been his inspiration for learning the French horn.

Outside in the square, the mechanical bell ringers struck nine, bringing us back to real time. Ruff's two hours were dwindling down. He closed the *Liber Usualis,* took his horn to the center of the church, stood under the central dome, and played "Were You There When They Crucified My Lord?" The great spiritual sounded as old and as majestic as the Gregorian chants, and it obviously had some of the same roots. When Ruff finished, the sacristan appeared, almost on the run, and I assumed that he was going to call a halt. *"Bene! Bene!"* he said, clapping his hands, trying to convey to Ruff the joy we could already see in his face. That the American spiritual had moved him even more deeply than the Gloria was a mystery too Byzantine to unravel; I only knew that it was no accident.

Ruff played three more spirituals. The first was "Steal Away to Jesus." The next was W. C. Handy's arrangement of "Give Me Jesus," which took me back to Ruff's Alabama boyhood town and the nearby log cabin where Handy had been born. The last was "Go Down, Moses," a pentatonic melody that could have come out of the *Liber Usualis* and that carries further emotional weight for anyone who knows its final words: "Let my people go."

The spirituals used up Ruff's remaining energy. He had been playing steadily for almost two hours. His tone had been beautiful throughout; he had played with care and control, respectful of the melody, but also with warmth. What he had just done was in many ways the summing up of his life. Dozens of unusual teachers had crossed his path and taught him what he needed to know next, but nobody had taught him more than he had taught himself. The fifty-one-year-old man in St. Mark's was the fifteen-year-old private who willed himself to learn the French horn in the boiler room of an army barracks in Cheyenne. The man who taught himself eight languages because of the doors they might unlock found that one of them could unlock the doors of St. Mark's. No interpreter could have opened those doors for him.

Ruff played one last melody, from a Bach cello suite, and put his horn back in its case. Except for a few candles the church was now dark. The sacristan told Ruff he would be glad to stay longer, but Ruff was through, and the sacristan said he would let us out. He blew out the candles in the nave and led us toward the back of the church. Ruff had prepared an *offerta,* and he gave it to the sacristan in two envelopes—one for him and one for the old monsignor. The sacristan took us through several corridors and rooms, turning out the lights and locking up behind him as he went, and finally brought us to a small door. He unbolted the door and gave us a warm Italian goodbye and we stepped out into the crowded streets of Venice.